THE ISLANDS OF IRELAND

Their Scenery, People, Life and Antiquities

By
THOMAS H. MASON
MEMBER OF THE ROYAL IRISH ACADEMY

*Illustrated from
Photographs by the Author*

Stenlake Publishing Ltd.

TO
MY WIFE
MY IDEAL COMPANION ON MANY OF MY
EXPEDITIONS AMONG THE
ISLANDS OF IRELAND
TO WHOM I AM INDEBTED FOR MUCH HELP
IN THE PREPARATION OF THIS BOOK

And somehow you're sick of the highway, with its noise and its easy needs,
And you seek the risk of the by-way, and you reck not where it leads.
The Lone Trail, Robert Service

Text and photographs © Thomas H. Mason, 1936.
First published in the United Kingdom, 1936,
by B. T. Batsford Ltd., London

Second edition 1938
Third edition 1950

Fourth edition 1967
by The Mercier Press, Cork

This fifth edition published 2023 by
Stenlake Publishing Ltd
54–58 Mill Square, Catrine,
Ayrshire, KA5 6RD.
01290 551122
www.stenlake.co.uk

Printed by Claro Print Ltd.
Offices 26/27, 1 Spiersbridge Way,
Glasgow, G46 8NG

ISBN 978-1-84033-947-5

**The publishers regret that they cannot supply
copies of any pictures featured in this book.**

Front cover: Steps to monastery, Skellig Michael.
Back cover: Dust jacket of the Batsford editions of *Islands of Ireland* featuring Brian Cook's painting of Granuaile's Castle, on Clare Island.

Publisher's Note to Fifth Edition

Thomas Holmes Mason of 39 Kenilworth Square, Dublin died on 12th February 1958 at the age of eighty, survived by his widow, Mrs Margaret Evelyn Mason and his four sons Standish, Alexander, Barry and Dermot. His obituaries recount an active life packed with many and varied interests. He was the head of the Mason optical firm, founded in 1780 and still in business today as Mason Technology Limited. An ancestor, Robert Mason, had been granted the freedom of the City of Dublin in 1712 and as a result Thomas Mason was a hereditary Honorary Freeman of the City of Dublin. The title died with him as the system was abolished by Lloyd George.

Thomas H. Mason

He began taking photographs at the age of 12 and by the time of his death had taken many thousands, of Ireland and elsewhere. The subject matter comprised landscapes, archaeology, birds, wildlife and social history, especially of the west of Ireland where many of his images were published as picture postcards under the Mason, Dublin imprint and sold in post offices and hotels. The postcard business had began with a series of cards of the Eucharistic Congress in Phoenix Park, but its mainstay became sepia photographic images of antiquities, scenery, hotels and Irish Life. All Mason postcards were produced directly from the negatives as photographic prints and the quality of the product was its downfall. When the price of silver increased, production became uneconomic and the postcard business was discontinued in the 1940s.

Mason photographs were also used to illustrate various Irish travel books such as *In Search of Ireland* by H V Morton. The entire photographic collection was lost in a fire in the 1960s.

Described by his friend, the journalist Malachy Hynes as "a slight little man 5' 7" tall, weighing 9st 7lbs with a ruddy complexion, a twinkle in his eye and a sense of humour as unquenchable as his non-stop cigarettes" Thomas Mason was patently a master of managing his time, with a long list of interests on top of his work and family commitments. He was a past president of the Irish Society for the Protection of Birds, the Irish National Trust (An Taisc), the Photography Society of Ireland, the Geographical Society of Ireland and the Dublin Naturalists' Field Club, president of the Dublin Mercantile Association and the Dublin Rotary Club. He was a member of the Dublin Zoological Council, the National Monuments' Council, and of the Council of the Royal Society of Antiquaries of Ireland. For all his work with these organisations he was elected to the Royal Irish Academy. An early interest was meteorology. At his Kenilworth Square home he kept records of sunshine and rain, wind speeds and temperature and provided long-range and surprisingly accurate weather forecasts to Irish newspapers. He was also a contributor to magazines on a variety of subjects.

Typical Mason social history postcards.

These scenes have been identified as being at Oughterard in County Galway but were published under the generic title of Irish Life, enabling a wider and more general sale.

Although this list of interests and activities is exhaustive it tells little of Mason's personality and character. For that we have to thank Malachy Hynes for the piece he wrote for The Irish Tatler And Sketch in its June 1948 edition simply entitled 'Thomas H. Mason. M.R.I.A.' Malachy recounts how when he came to Dublin' "after sixteen years roving" he "didn't like it one bit", but it grew on him as he gradually got to know people, and the very first of these was Thomas Mason.

> "The very first Dubliner I got to know had, simmering within him, elements of Gaelic, Cromwellian and Ulster-Scot, and his sons, whom I got to know as well as himself, were an amalgam of Pictish, Scottish, Danish and Swedish alloys. Still, after some 250 years growing in Dublin's sociological skillet, the whole thing boiled down to as fine, as tasty, as wholesome and nourishing a brand of Irishry as ever I did savour".

Hynes came to know the Masons through a common interest in photography and was a frequent visitor to the Mason firm's Dame Street premises, around which he was allowed to wander freely and get to know the entire staff from the glass-blowers to the instrument repairers. The visits were therapeutic too:

> "No matter how much the world for me is out of kilter, a few minutes chat with the brains of the whole movement will put it back on its axis again and I'll know for certain I made no mistake in coming back to Ireland. All sorts of people come up to have a yarn with Mr. Mason, who they regard as one of their best habits. Down the country they have an expression for such visits - cuiairds - just an old Irish neighbourly custom".

Likening Mason to Oliver Goldsmith Hynes recounts all his interests plus what he describes as *"the supreme hobby of collecting characters"*. According to Hynes Mason could lecture with authority on many subjects but never came across as a know-it-all.

Malachy's article then delves extensively into the Mason family history and blood lines to demonstrate the diversity which Mason himself was so proud of, acknowledging that his family's Saxon origins had been *"purified or polluted according to point of view"* and mischievously proclaiming *"The cleverest and most companionable dog I ever possessed was one of mixed ancestry!"* Malachy Hynes' conclusion was that Thomas Mason, the man, was a melting pot and typical of many of the old Dublin families :

> "look at him: look at all the ingredients that went into the makings of this so typical Irishman and you'll learn more about the construction of the Irish race at a glance than you would up at the National Library after wearing out many pairs of Tommy Mason's spectacles."

The following information about Thomas Mason's photographic work for the firm is reproduced from notes provided by the Mason family to the late Norman Cullen of Belfast, who was an avid collector of Mason postcards.

> "The business was very small at the time he joined and his father allowed him to dabble in his hobby of photography. At that time he used a half-plate wooden camera which held a total of six plates and it was the limitation of six plates which could only be loaded in the dark that concentrated his skills so that he made the best use of each shot. The photographic department, when he joined the business, only sold photographic equipment and chemicals

for processing. The developing and printing only came when Kodak invented roll film and it became available in the late 1890's. He started accumulating his library of negatives at an early age and gradually built up the collection to a total of 8,000 photographs, some of which had been taken by his father.

Most of the photographs were taken with an old style wooden camera with half plate negative glass plates. As a young single man he would travel around the country on his bicycle, usually with a couple of friends and they camped at various locations. When he got married his photography trips were greatly curtailed. He did, however, manage a few trips to the Saltee Islands with some of his friends. He'd had to wait until his sons grew up before he could seriously take up photography again. He bought a Model T Ford and the first thing he did was to take the whole family to the Saltees.

In the 1930's the railway companies had photographs, depicting scenes of their areas, displayed in the carriages. These photographs were published by Lawrence of Dublin. They were all taken before 1914 and had gone out of date. Masons used to print the photographs for Lawrence. They had a library of negatives, but didn't have developing and printing facilities at all. The railway companies eventually asked Masons to take over the photography for them. This was around 1934 and quite a lot of gaps had to be filled. Mr Mason was 57 at this time and along with his son Alex went off to Galway. They took many film packs with them, went straight to Galway and worked around the coast photographing places and things which were not in their library. They generally worked from early morning till late at night. The last thing to do was to change the plates to be ready for the next day's work. The equipment was carried in a large trunk with wooden handles. They often took an eiderdown with them, which was more suitable than blankets for darkening the hotel window to facilitate the changing of the plates.

When his sons got up into their 20's Mr Mason started taking his wife with him on his photography expeditions. He got a new Fiat car which had a top speed of about 45 mph, but it was a good, steady, solid car. His next car was a Model A Ford which was lockable and therefore good for the security of the equipment.

Mason's Model A Ford had a cameo role in some of the firm's postcard views.

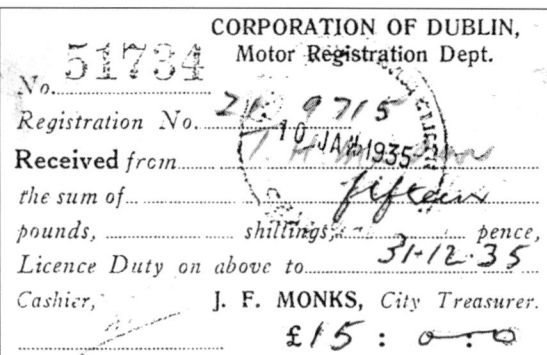

Motor Registration for ZI9715

Centre: Mason's Model A at Woodenbridge Hotel, Co. Wicklow.

Bottom: His next car, a Ford V8. The lady next to the car is believed to be Mrs Mason.

His next car was a Ford V8 [Model 60, UK version of the American Model 48] which he drove all over the country. Because he had someone to look after the business for him he was able to take many photography trips, some of which lasted 6 to 8 weeks.

It was well known that his collection was better than the Lawrence collection which was really dated, having been taken before 1914 and of practically every town and village in the country. His street scenes were very good but he had not taken up-to-date photographs at all. The premises that the Lawrence photographer operated from was in O'Connell Street and was burned down in the 1916 troubles. After that the Masons did all of Lawrence's prints. Mr Mason knew Mr Willie Lawrence quite well.

5 and 6 Dame Street,
Thomas Mason's Dublin premises

Mr Mason took a lot of photographs recording archaeological works, monuments, Irish Crosses, round towers etc. He photographed a great many interesting things like the beehive cells on the Skelligs and the ruined churches of Co Galway and the Aran Islands.

Many of his photographs were reproduced in the book he wrote which was published in 1936, called *The Islands of Ireland*. In fact there are 160 photographs in the book, some of which have been produced as postcards. His son Alex accompanied him on his trips to many of the Islands. Some of the Islanders did not like having their photograph taken but Mr Mason, on such occasions, used a reflex camera with a right-angled prism so that the camera was not pointed directly at the people and they were not aware that they had been photographed.

When Alex took over the postcard side of the business he had his father's lists of where and what he had to photograph. He would take photographs of important hotels because this gave him an introduction. The hotels would buy the cards and use them for advertising. They would buy a couple of thousand. Then they would order another couple of thousand during the season. Mr Mason didn't like this. After one of his trips he sat down at home with Alex to decide what to publish. He had some lovely photographs of sand dunes. They were exquisite but there wasn't an hotel within miles and you couldn't take photographs of sand dunes just anywhere. Alex said he wouldn't publish them. They had an awful row. Mrs Mason was coming up with tea for them and when she heard the din she just went back down the stairs again and left them to it.

On the evening of 25th May 1965 the firm's premises at 5 and 6 Dame Street were destroyed by fire. The optics and photographic departments moved to temporary premises at 50 Dawson Street and subsequently in April 1967 to 32 Dawson Street. Both of these departments were closed in 1972."

The Fire 25th May 1965

After his death Thomas Mason's book *The Islands of Ireland* was referred to as *"a classic of its kind"*, *"a best-seller"* and *"still a standard work"*. It was first published in 1936 in hardback by B.T. Batsford Ltd. with a delightful dust-jacket illustration in pastel colours by Brian Cook and copiously illustrated with the author's photographs. The book was written in 1935 when Mason was convalescing from a bout of pneumonia. Until then his *"greatest difficulty in life"* it was said was *"to compel himself to sit down for more than about two minutes at the one given time, in any of the various places to which his extraordinarily-active brain propels him during his thronged day."* The pneumonia compelled Mason to sit down, so he used the time to compile the book. The first edition was quickly followed by a second edition in 1938 and a third in the Spring of 1950. In March 1967 the book, substantially redesigned, was published as a small paperback by The Mercier Press of Cork. Mason's photographs were not included and instead the book's cover and the line drawing illustrations inside the book were by the Dutch-born Cor Klaasen who by this time was a prolific illustrator and had become an Irish citizen.

Cover of Mercier Press' fourth edition of the *Islands of Ireland*.

Thomas Mason's photograph of the steps to the monastry on Skelig Michael (Great Skellig).

Note to Third Edition

SINCE the second edition of this book was published, there have been many changes in the islands.

The passing of the years has taken its toll, and a number of my old friends have passed on. I must mention a few of them: Dr. Robin Flower, Tomas O'Crohan of Blasket Island, my hosts on Inishmore Aran, Mr. and Mrs. McDonagh, and several others-may they rest in peace.

The pressure of economic conditions has caused the evacuation of Inishmurray and reduced the population of Gt. Blasket Island to about half of its pre-war numbers. Many of the former inhabitants have obtained holdings on the adjacent mainland, but there has also been the emigration of the younger folk to distant lands, which has been a feature of island life for many years.

A change has also taken place in the bird population of the Great Saltee. The calculation of the number of birds was originally made by the late Professor J. A. Scott and myself in 1911. Since then the puffins have decreased enormously, and a recent census in 1949 by a group of ornithologists gives a total of about 50,000 birds. I believe this is an under-estimate and that my calculation was an over-estimate, but there is still a very large population for such a small island.

Thomas H. Mason,
Winter 1949-50

Preface and Acknowledgments

SOME time ago I was honoured by an invitation to lecture on 'The Islands of Ireland' before the members of the Royal Dublin Society. This lecture was so favourably received that I have been tempted to write it down, and this book is the result of my efforts. In the following pages I have amplified what I said in my lecture and have added a considerable amount of fresh material which I have obtained in subsequent expeditions.

Although the title of this book is *The Islands of Ireland* it does not profess to deal with all the islands of the Irish coast. I am aware that some of those which are not included, Aranmore, County Donegal, and a number of islands off the Mayo, Galway, Kerry and Cork shores are worthy of mention, and even some which are included (for instance, Lambay and Rathlin) deserve more space than could be allotted to them.

There are at least a hundred islands off the Irish coast, many of them inhabited. I have heard that there are 365, one for every day of the year, but I have never had sufficient patience to count them; and even if I were sufficiently industrious to attempt to do so, I would find it difficult to know from maps which were mere rocks and which could legitimately be termed islands.

In making the selection I have been guided by two main considerations: first, the desire not to curtail unduly the description of those islands which are the most important and interesting, and secondly, the limitations of space which are inevitable if a book of this nature is to be produced with ample illustrations and at a moderate price.

My thanks are due to my many friends who live on the islands and without whose friendship I could not have obtained much of the information recorded in these pages. Thanks are also due to the Council of the Royal Irish Academy for permission to reproduce the illustration of early maps showing the position of Hy Brasil, and to Dr. H. O'Neill Hencken of the Harvard University Archaeological Mission for permission to publish the photograph of a dug-out canoe discovered in the course of his excavations of Ballinderry No. 2 Crannoge. I am indebted to the late Mr. J. J. Buckley, M.R.I.A., for the suggestion that the wrecks of the Spanish Armada on the west of Ireland were due to incorrect maps, and also to Mr. M. D. Westropp, M.R.I.A., of Dublin, who helped me to obtain a photograph of an early map bearing on this subject.

I would also like to express my acknowledgment to the Proprietors of *Punch* for permission to print a portion of an ode *To a Cormorant* which appeared in an issue of that periodical. The photographs of an Aran cradle and basket were taken by Mr. A. Dodds of Dublin. The photographs of 'Island Rockscape,' Aran, and of mural paintings on Clare Island were taken by the late Dr. Fogarty of Limerick. The photograph of the coracle on the River Boyne was taken by the late Mr. A. M. Geddes of Dublin. All the other illustrations are reproduced from photographs taken by my sons and myself.

I would recommend those of my readers who are interested in archaeological and historical details to consult the *Antiquarian Handbook*, No. VI, published by the Royal Society of Antiquaries of Ireland, to which publication I am indebted for some of the historical matter embodied in this book.

Thomas H. Mason
Dublin,
Autumn, 1936

Himself and Herself, Inishmaan, Aran

Contents

Chapters

One	Introductory	15
Two	The East Coast	19
Three	Poteen	21
Four	Tory Island, County Donegal	23
Five	Island Boats	33
Six	Inishmurray, County Sligo	43
Seven	Achill Island, County Mayo	51
Eight	Clare Island, County Mayo	63
Nine	Inishbofin, County Galway	71
Ten	The Aran Islands, County Galway	77
Eleven	Antiquities On The Aran Islands	89
Twelve	Music, Marriage, Etc., On The Aran Islands	103
Thirteen	Inishere, Aran	119
Fourteen	The Blasket Islands, County Kerry	123
Fifteen	The Skelligs, County Kerry	139
Sixteen	The Saltee Island, County Wexford	149
Seventeen	Conclusion	165

Index	166

Chapter One

Introductory

I learnt at school, and the dictionary confirms the statement, that 'an island is a mass of land surrounded by water.' This dictum is true even if, as in the case of Achill and some other Irish islands, there is a bridge connecting it to the mainland and one can drive across the Atlantic, or at least a portion of it, in a car.

I am not sure why islands possess such a fascination for many people, but the fact remains that they do. Artists, literary men and even millionaires, take up their abode on isolated islands and find there a retreat from the clamour and din of modern civilisation, where their spirits can expand, and where the primitive virtues and values of mankind are not swamped in a material world which has, to a large extent, lost its soul. The early Celtic Church realised the soul value of these lonely places and on many of the islands off the coast of Ireland the remains of their early settlements may be seen.

I spend the greater portion of my conscious hours in the city of Dublin where one has to keep the doors and windows closed – otherwise one could not hear oneself talking, the noise is so great. The telephone bell is ringing all day, motor-horns are hooting and everybody is in a hurry. If one wants to cross the road considerable dexterity is required if it is not to be one's last crossing.

These remarks apply to almost every modern city. I have watched the people in the London tubes rushing to catch a train – another train would be there in a couple of minutes, and yet the crowds rush as if it were the last train to heaven. I have never known

Interior of the Cashel, Inishmurray, showing the men's cemetery, Altoir Beg, Clocha-Breaca, Toory Brennell (School-house), Teampul-na-Teindh (Church of the Fire) Teach Molaise and Teampul Molaise. Part of the early monastic settlement on the island.

the spiritual value of solitude so much as when on one occasion I sat for some hours on the high peak of Skellig Michael, just above the remains of the early Christian Monastery, and drank in the sunshine six hundred feet above the Atlantic, with the whole glorious panorama of the Kerry Mountains before me. But even in other islands which are inhabited one can generally get the solitude which is such a balm, and in any case one is free of motor-cars and telephones. In some islands even wheeled vehicles are not in evidence.

It may be a far cry to Venice, but I cannot help mentioning that on the only occasion on which I visited that Mecca of Northern Italy I was greatly impressed by the absence of noise. I saw only one wheeled vehicle – it was a perambulator and the infant was asleep. The authorities in that city have wisely regulated the use of motor-boats in the Grand Canal, for, if they were allowed to run wild, a great amount of the charm of Venice would disappear. One requires peace to enjoy to the full the artistic treasures of that beautiful city.

In some of the inhabited islands of Ireland, in an especial degree in the Aran and Blasket Islands, I have found a courtesy that is impossible to describe; the inhabitants may now be peasants, but they are the remnants of ancient races and are gentlefolk in the literal and highest meaning of that phrase. I shall never forget a conversation that I had on the steamer with an Aran man who was going to Galway Fair to sell a cow. He asked me how I had liked my holiday in Aran, and when I replied that I had enjoyed it immensely, mentioning casually that I found the people so courteous, he turned towards me with a look of astonishment and said, 'Well, and isn't it a proper thing to be kindly to strangers?'

I felt ashamed of myself. Here was a peasant living on what somebody has described as a barren rock in the Atlantic Ocean stating a fundamental Christian axiom which is too often forgotten in these days of intense materialism, and he was astonished that I should have mentioned it as a fact worthy of notice.

More than one person has expressed to me the fear that the publicity given to the islands in recent years by books and films will make them popular as tourist resorts and destroy the finer characteristics of the people. Undoubtedly excessive 'tourism' does tend in this direction, but in the case of the islanders I do not think this will occur; their fundamentals are too deeply engrained, and the class of tourist who will go to the islands is of necessity a class with the finer instincts. I cannot visualise the type which enjoys Blackpool or the Isle of Man forsaking these resorts and vulgarising the Blaskets. No! Blackpool is quite safe for my lifetime at any rate.

Some of my own circle of suburban acquaintances have commiserated with my wife and cannot understand how she could find any pleasure in going to these 'awful' places with her husband. They look on me as a freak and my wife as a martyr. They do not realise that she has an instinct for the finer things of life and they know not what they miss.

I do not suggest that these islanders are all saints. They are not. There is, however, probably a larger proportion of potential saints among them than you will get in Putney or Rathmines. They are ordinary human beings of flesh and blood, without much artificiality. Family ties are beautiful and strong, and if they do have feuds these are generally between different families over matters which to us may appear small, but to them are important and sometimes vital.

One writer, in his book on the Aran Islands, features – as the movie people say – their drinking bouts. He was not a teetotaller himself and had no excuse except the artistic temperament, but when one realises the lives of hardship these islanders live, their incessant struggle to wring a subsistence, or rather an existence, from bare rocks and angry seas, and the monotony of their lives throughout a great portion of the year, one can excuse their occasional lapses. Which of us, in similar conditions, would be as temperate? 'He that is without sin let him first cast a stone.' Personally I can only remember once having seen a drunken man, and I have spent lengthy periods on all of the islands which are the subject of this book.

The books which have appeared in recent years dealing with Irish island life have been written by natives of the islands – with the exception of J. M. Synge's masterpiece, which was written forty years ago. They are wonderful pieces of literature, compiled from inside knowledge of conditions that are fast passing away, while I write as an outsider who has felt the warmth of an island welcome and has done his best to record both with the camera and the pen what he feels will be interesting in future years.

The islands have many interests – the life of the people, folklore, traditions, archaeology and bird life, all subjects which really deserve separate books to themselves. Times are changing, and even in the islands these changes are visible since I first knew them nearly fifty years ago; the progress of changing conditions tends to accelerate, and possibly in another fifty years there will not be the same wealth of material.

The visitor to an island must not make the error of mistaking natural courtesy for a sense of inferiority; it is widely different, in fact I would go so far as to say that the inferiority complex should be with the visitor. If he repays courtesy with courtesy and respects the island-man as one man should respect another, he will have nothing but pleasant memories and will learn much. If, on the other hand, he feels and shows a sense of superiority he will have a dull time and learn nothing. These people 'size one up' very accurately, and if they feel that you are attempting to patronise them the door is closed.

Above everything else, one should never offer money except for actual work done; but one can always offer tobacco or cigarettes; they are presents that one gentleman can accept

Razorbills, Saltee Island.

from another. I also found that, when one had gained their friendship, the islanders were delighted to get photographs of the family which they could send to their relatives in the USA, particularly if, as was frequently the case, there were young children who were born after the older children had emigrated. Every household, without exception, has relatives abroad. If for any reason the photographs were a failure I always wrote stating the fact; one should always faithfully keep one's promises to them. On subsequent visits – even after a lapse of ten years – I was received with a warm welcome in houses where they remembered me as the 'little thin gentleman' who had sent them the photographs.

With regard to accommodation, some of the islands have small hotels, in others I have camped or lodged in cottages, and in every case I found the latter spotlessly clean. I prefer to stay in the cottages as in that way one gets to know the people in a more intimate manner, and the fireside evening talks, with generally a couple of neighbours present in addition to the family, are always full of interest.

I remember as a youth that when I wanted to camp on Dalkey Island near Dublin my parents squashed the idea – would certainly be late for business every morning, or if the sea were rough I might be drowned. I was an only son, the fifth generation in our firm, and consequently precious, so I had to be content with camping on a peninsula. A few years later when, during my holidays, I camped on Inishmore Island, Aran, County Galway, what I saw there made a great impression on me. I was 'bitten' even as a young man, and frequently visited the other islands. The islands never lost their fascination for me, and as the years rolled on and I have arrived at middle age I realise more and more their tonic effect, mental, physical and spiritual.

The names of the islands on the east coast of Ireland, and indeed of many places on the mainland, are of Scandinavian origin, and are monuments in the present day to the great part that the Viking invaders played in the history of Ireland in pre-Norman times – Wexford, Arklow, Wicklow, Dalkey, Howth, Ireland's Eye, Lambay, Carlingford, Strangford, are all Scandinavian place-names. Even in the north of County Dublin there is a district called Fingal (Fair Foreigner, i.e. Norseman) and a village called Baldoyle – Ballydhugal (the Town of the Black Foreigner, i.e. the Dane). The Fingal men are still great sailors and will be found on ships in all parts of the world. The Viking raids were first made on the islands; Lambay Island, County Dublin, was first visited in AD 795, and nearly every island on the coast of Ireland was raided in the following two centuries. The terror inspired by these pirates can still be traced in the language of the ordinary people- the expression 'an ould Dane' describes a terribly unpleasant person. The ruination of an ancient building is likewise always credited either to 'the Danes' or Cromwell, even though the structure may not have been in existence at the time of the Vikings or may have been in ruins before Cromwell's time.

Those islands which harboured the monastic settlements of the early Celtic Church were given special attention and were raided on numerous occasions. The Vikings eventually made settlements which became the trading ports of the country, for the ancient Irish were not a commercial people. Our capital city of Dublin was originally a Viking settlement. My father used to say that Dublin was never an Irish city until the Tipperary men, who were publicans in the city, captured the Corporation. After the Norman Conquest the descendants of the Vikings became the commercial community of Ireland. Although the Vikings raided the west coast they do not appear to have made permanent settlements there (with the exception of Limerick), the Roman Empire never conquered Ireland, and the result is that we have in the Islands of the West a culture and tradition which extend to very early times.

Chapter Two

The East Coast

Dalkey Island and Ireland's Eye, both in County Dublin, contain the remains of early churches; the former also has the remains of a fort built during the Napoleonic period, and whilst they are pleasant places for picnics for the citizens of Dublin, these islands are otherwise not of much interest. Lambay Island is the private property of Lord Revelstoke, whose father built a fine residence on it and who resides there for some months every year. As it is private property indiscriminate landing is not allowed; previous permission must be obtained.

It is full of interest. The late and the present Lord Revelstoke have made it a sanctuary for wild life – the first in Ireland – and myriads of sea birds resort to it during the nesting season. The peregrine falcon and the raven, free from the attentions of marauding egg collectors, rear their young here regularly.

Dalkey Island Church.

Some years ago Dublin workmen who were employed on the island during repairs to the residence, after two nights of terror, insisted on sleeping on the mainland, protesting that the island was haunted and that nothing would induce them to spend another night on it. The sounds they had heard were, however, capable of a natural explanation. Amongst the numerous species of birds nesting on the island is the Manx shearwater. These sea birds only come to land during the nesting season, when they nest in holes, the parents taking turns on the nest. One of the birds is fishing all day and returns late at night, heralding its return in a most riotous manner with blood-curdling cries which could be best described as a cross between a donkey's bray and a cock's crow. The birds being invisible in the dark, the workmen refused to believe that this nerve-shattering noise could be caused by any creature of this world. I can quite sympathise with these city dwellers, as I remember the shock I received when I first heard the noise at close quarters on a pitch dark night. In the Eastern Mediterranean it is believed that the shearwaters are possessed by the souls of the damned.

It is fascinating to watch from the tall cliffs the playful antics of the seals which, being protected, are much less shy here than in most places. The enlightened policy of Lord Revelstoke is amply rewarded by the presence of the wild creatures and birds who have security within a distance of about fifteen miles from a city of nearly half a million inhabitants. The rocks are mostly of volcanic origin, although the principal rock of the mainland is carboniferous limestone.

The earliest inhabitants of Ireland dwelt on the shores and adjoining islands, the mainland being probably covered with forests and swamps. On Lambay, during the progress of harbour works in recent years, fine implements dating from Neolithic and Bronze Age times (3000-500 BC) have been discovered in the raised beach on the west side of the island. The occupation of this site extended even to historic times, as the discovery of Saxon remains at a higher level, would indicate. Archaeological excavation on Lambay Island would probably lead to discoveries of great interest. I myself have seen dozens of flaked flints projecting in an open section and have also seen worked flints brought to the surface by burrowing rabbits at the north end of the island.

Rathlin Island, off the north-east corner of Antrim, has richly rewarded the scientists who have paid so much attention to it. Flint is abundant, and evidence goes to prove that a flourishing Neolithic industry had existed in this district. This industry, on account of its magnitude, was evidently of an export nature; in fact the island and the adjoining coast of County Antrim would appear to have held in the late Stone Age the position that Detroit holds at present in the motor age.

In Elizabethan times the island was the scene of a great slaughter. The Antrim Chiefs, who were fighting the English Crown forces, sent the old people, women and children to the island for safety, but the English fleet sailed from Belfast and slaughtered every living person. After this holocaust the island was uninhabited for many years.

When one stands on the north-east corner of the island it is hard to realise that one is in Ireland, the Scottish coast appearing almost as near as the mainland of Ireland; and indeed one realises when speaking to the islanders that they are even more Scottish than Irish. Their accent is a cross between Northern Irish and Lowland Scots. They enlist in the Scottish regiments and there is much coming and going between both mainlands. This interchange follows the prehistoric movements, as there is no doubt that the first settlers came to Ireland via the narrow sea of the North Channel, and later raids and plantations were carried out by distant kinsmen of the earlier inhabitants.

Most of us when at school learned the story of Robert Bruce and the spider, and how Bruce, when in hiding, was encouraged by the perseverance of the spider to the further efforts which finally gained him the Scottish Crown. The moral was pointed as a tribute to the Scottish character, so I take great pleasure in explaining to my Scottish friends that Bruce was of Norman descent and the spider was Irish. This episode took place in a cave which is still to be seen on Rathlin Island.

All that is left of Bruce's Castle, Rathlin Island, Co. Antrim.

CHAPTER THREE

Poteen

Before dealing with the islands on the west coast, I would like to correct the popular impression that it is on these islands that poteen (illicit whisky) is distilled. It is true that on some of the uninhabited islands next the mainland poteen is made, but the principal seat of the industry is among the bogs and mountains of County Donegal and County Galway. It forms, however, one of the 'invisible imports' of the islands, where its consumption, owing to the ban of the Church and the activity of the police, is largely decreasing. The poteen traffic is an unmitigated evil, but it is hard to blame many of the distillers, for without the money they get from the sale of this poison they would be unable to exist. If economic conditions were better the manufacture would probably decrease so much that it would be comparatively negligible.

I became aware of the poteen traffic on only one of the numerous islands that I have visited. From a distance we could see a thin column of blue smoke ascending from the foreshore, but this disappeared as we approached. When our bags were being taken from the boat, one of the islanders asked what was the meaning of them, so I mentioned that we wished to stay on the island and was told that there was no accommodation. I was surprised at this reception, because, as an unknown visitor, I had received warm welcomes on other islands, and this experience was new to me.

One of the boatmen in a whisper told me to wait, as he might be able to arrange matters, so I contented myself by sitting on a wall for about half an hour until the boatman came back with the principal man of the island, who informed me that he would put us up. Afterwards I discovered the cause of their reluctance to accept us: poteen is distilled on the island. The smoke which we saw from the sea came from a still, and the islanders had suspicions that we might be spies.

The boatman who cleared my character, although he had never seen me previously, was a retired policeman, but even then we were not altogether trusted.

I saw in our bedroom a photograph of a doctor whom I knew well and, on mentioning the fact to my host, we were immediately placed on a different footing. We were now accepted as friends and perfect confidence was at once established. The doctor had been one of an excursion party to the island at a time when a member of the household was seriously ill, and he remained on the island until the patient was out of danger. That incident occurred more than thirty years ago, but the doctor is still remembered with the greatest affection.

When their confidence was gained the islanders spoke freely to me and I even saw a still, which was on the foreshore in 'no man's land' so that if discovered in a raid by the police nobody could be held responsible for it. Poteen has been made here for generations, and the people think the Government are very unjust in trying to suppress their principal industry. The soil is scanty and poor, and except for lobster fishing, which occupies them for a few months in the summer, they have no other means of obtaining the ready money which they require for the purchase of necessities. They look on illicit distilling as a legitimate occupation on their island, but think it should be abolished on the mainland. One man told me that during the war they made plenty of money, but afterwards, 'when there was no law or order, they were making poteen everywhere,' he said. 'That wasn't right, and had to be stopped.'

He also said that 'the ould police' (Royal Irish Constabulary) were decent men. 'If they knew ye were in the middle of a run they would give ye time to finish it before they

An illicit still for distilling poteen.

raided ye, but ye can't trust them new police at all.' The British tried to stop distilling by putting police on the island, 'but,' said my informant, 'they got that fond of it sure they were making it themselves in a few months' – which statement may not be strictly accurate.

One of the islanders 'did' six months in jail because poteen was found in his house. His wife told mine the story of the seizure. Before retiring for the night it was her duty to remove any poteen from the house and hide it amongst the boulders on the shore. It was a 'dirty' night of rain and wind and she was confident there would be no raid in such bad weather. At three o'clock in the morning they were awakened by loud knocks on the door. 'Oh, Sean,' she said to her husband, 'we are lost. I never put out the poteen.' 'And would ye believe me,' she concluded, 'he never said a cross word to me but got up and let in the police; the poteen was found and they took him away to jail for six months. When he came home he never cast it up to me again.' He surely is a husband to be treasured.

The husband told me the story of his experience in court: 'They fined others ten pounds, but they fined me fifty. It wasn't fair. If they had fined me ten pounds, aye, or even fifteen, I would have paid it, but I would not pay fifty, so they had to feed me for six months and they got no money; it was bad business, Mr. Mason.' I quite agree.

I heard many exciting stories about the 'running' of cargoes to the mainland and was brought back in imagination to the days of my boyhood, when I read stirring tales about smugglers and contraband cargoes.

Chapter Four

Tory

Tory Island lies off the north-west corner of Donegal about seven miles from the mainland. My wife and myself crossed in the post boat, a stout vessel equipped with a Kelvin engine, for the winds and sea on this angle of the Atlantic are notoriously bad. No boat had been able to cross for ten days, but we were assured that the storm was over so we took our courage in our hands. The passage took half an hour longer than usual, and I had to wedge myself into a corner and hold firmly to iron bolts to prevent myself being thrown about. Even with these precautions I was bruised and sore, so that I can only thank heaven that it was not what the boatmen call a rough sea.

A number of the islanders were waiting the arrival of the boat, and our luggage, which included a number of small cases containing photographic equipment, was seized upon and carried to the small hotel without any thought of reward. I could not help contrasting this with the more sophisticated tourist resorts. I was at a loss to reciprocate until I thought of sweets for the children. Three pennyworth of sweets established me firmly in their favour.

Tory – which is pronounced with a short 'o' – is one of the most desolate and yet one of the most interesting islands. It is composed of hard siliceous rocks with a very thin covering of soil; the peat is nearly all gone and the island is being rapidly denuded of its pasturage, which is being cut away for use as fuel. Even on the common, which is reserved for grazing, I saw large strips of naked rock where the surface 'scraw' had been removed. I hesitate to think of the future of the inhabitants if this denudation is not checked. Emigration is necessary; there is not a subsistence for the large families which are usual, and their emigration is not to the USA, as is common everywhere else in Ireland, it is to Scotland.

Cliffs and tors, Tory Island.

The inhabitants all speak Irish; many of them 'have' no English. My wife, having thanked a woman who had gone out of her way to do her some small service – the woman 'had' very little English and it was difficult to understand what she said – got the reply: 'Why should you thank me? Sure I am learning the English all the time from you.'

I have met the same eagerness to learn English in all the Irish-speaking districts. Emigration is an economic necessity and without English they realise that they cannot make a living outside the Gaeltacht. One man told me that he had worked in a foundry in Glasgow but got into bad health and came home, adding that he 'got good money, but what is the use of it if you don't get your health?' – a statement that might, with advantage, be taken to heart by many modern business men.

Like most of the western islands Tory is treeless, and the side facing the Atlantic is bounded by high cliffs. These cliffs are worn into fantastic pillars of rock or tors, from which the island takes its name. I need hardly say the name has no connection with a modern political party.

The island is in the track of North Atlantic shipping and wrecks are, or rather were, frequent. The Commissioners of Irish Lights have now established a Marconi direction-finding station, and it is to be hoped that shipping casualties will be reduced.

These wrecks played an important part in the economics of the islanders. Everywhere one sees portions of iron ships – the hearths are 'tiled' with iron plates, foot-bridges over drains outside the cottages are composed of iron plates and I even saw a home-made harrow whose teeth were ships' bolts. One man, pointing out the remains of a ship which had struck fifteen months previously, said it was a grand wreck; it had carried a cargo of flour which lasted the islanders for more than a year. 'Ah,' he said, ''tis time there was another wreck, there was no want in the island then.'

The islanders look upon flotsam and jetsam as their legitimate property – they are only defrauding the Government, which is not a crime but rather a virtue in the eyes of most Irishmen – but they make heroic efforts to save the lives of the shipwrecked mariners. Some time before my visit they had climbed down the cliffs and, by means of ropes, had rescued with great difficulty and risk the crew of a small collier.

Nowhere have I seen agriculture carried on with such primitive implements. Ploughs are home-made, composed of wood shod with iron retrieved from wrecks; harrows are made of wood and iron bolts from ships; the crops are cut by sickle or scythe and are threshed with the flail, which consists of two sticks fastened together by a leather thong. Considerable skill is required to use the flail if one is to avoid being struck by the swinging end. The grain when separated is winnowed on a circular riddle, called locally a 'wyte.' This has no holes but is composed simply of sheepskin with a twisted straw rope forming the rim.

There are one or two wheeled vehicles, but the principal method of conveyance is the slide cart – a cart without wheels but with iron-shod runners projecting from the rear, which slide along the ground. The photograph on the facing page shows the construction better than words can describe it. It may also be noticed that the harness is made of straw ropes plaited together.

One can see these carts tilted against the side of many of the houses. I could not fathom their use, and it was only when I saw one with a horse harnessed to it that I realised what it was. I believe some of these carts may still be found in districts in the Mourne Mountains, County Down, but I do not think that anywhere else will one find so many of these actual survivals in everyday use.

The inhabitants of Tory frequently live to a great age. At the time of my visit one man was a hundred years old and was looking for another wife. In former years they elected

Threshing with a flail, Tory Island.

Slide cart with load, Tory Island.

Primitive plough and harrows, Tory Island.

a 'king.' The last king was a very small man, as his tiny chair indicates, and he must have possessed a powerful personality to compensate for his diminutive stature.

It is easy to understand persistence of tradition and the spoken word in a long-living, primitive and isolated community, and nowhere have I observed this emphasised so strongly as on Tory Island. Prehistoric myths and legends are mixed up with events of medieval history and recent happenings, and the whole jumble is narrated as if it were a single tale of the occurrences of a few years ago. The predominating figure of the mythology of the island is Balor, the God Chief of the Fomorians, a race of legendary pirates who inhabited the island in early times and from their stronghold scourged the rest of Ireland with their depredations. Balor was a most unpleasant gentleman; he had an eye, like Cyclops, in the front of his head, and so wicked was he that an angry glance from his single eye was sufficient to slay the beholder. When his eye became tired in battle the eyelid was held up by means of ropes and pulleys so that his followers would not lose the advantage of his deadly glance.

He represents in Irish mythology the Powers of Darkness in contrast with his grandson Lugh, by whom he was finally slain and whose 'Sword of Light' forms the design on one of our Irish Free State postal stamps. Lugh was the God of Light in Gaul and in Ireland, and has left his traces in many place-names on the Continent, such as Lugudunum (Leyden), Lyons, etc. The story of Balor and Lugh is one of the Celtic classics and is presented in a most readable form in the scholarly work of the late T. W. Rolleston, entitled *Myths and Legends of the Celtic Race*.

The east end of the island is known as the 'dun' (pronounced doon), and is separated from the larger portion by a narrow neck. Earthen fortifications are still visible, and it is probable that a prehistoric cliff fort existed here. It certainly was a fortress even in the seventeenth century, as it was here that the last stand of the O'Donnells was made against the forces of the English Crown. A small hoard of Elizabethan silver coins which was found here in 1931 was evidently an echo of this conflict. The woman who found them believed them to be Balor's money – an interesting sidelight on the dominating figure of Balor in the traditions of the Island.

A keg of 'bog' butter had also been found in the process:.. of cutting turf. When I mentioned the matter to an old man he explained that robbers had lived in the 'dun' some time ago. They were, he said, bad men, who, when the island men were out fishing, used to steal the butter and fish from the women, who then adopted the plan of hiding it in the bog. 'We had no peace,' he said, 'until the police (?) came and they shot one there and another there' (pointing to the places), 'and then,' said he, 'we had peace.' The bog butter was probably two hundred years old, but the old man told the story as if the events had occurred a few years previously.

St. Columcille is the dominating figure of the Christian legends, even as Balor dominates the pagan traditions. We find traces of St. Columcille in many islands. He is recorded as having lived in Lambay, Rathlin, Tory and Inishmurray, and his missionary establishment on the island of Iona, off the west coast of Scotland, was the chief means of converting the Scots to Christianity.

I was told the story of the coming of St. Columcille to Tory. The saint was standing on the top of Muckish, a mountain in County Donegal which is more than two thousand feet in height. His eyes roamed the landscape seeking a place where he could build a church, but there were many places where the people were badly in need of his ministrations, so, being unable to make up his mind, after prolonged prayer he took a javelin and threw it. Where the javelin fell he would build a church.

It landed in Tory Island – a miraculous throw, as the island is about fifteen miles from Muckish. The spot where the javelin fell is still pointed out. This is a large crater-like hole near the northern cliffs, about seventy feet deep and fifty yards wide at the top, narrowing considerably towards the bottom where the sea enters through a hole in the base of the cliff. The islanders regard this spot with awe and will not approach it in the dark.

Some years ago an American visitor climbed down the steeply sloping side, intending to read his book in a spot where he was protected from the wind. He read for some time and then fell asleep in the warm sunshine. When he awoke all the sunshine was gone. He already felt the chill of the evening air and started to climb up the steep slope, but having a wooden leg he found that he was unable to do so and shouted for help. The nearest cottage is some distance away and the woman of the house, hearing the noises, came to the conclusion that they were caused by 'sheegees' (fairies) and was afraid to leave her house. So the unfortunate American spent the night in the cavity and was rescued only on the following day by a man who came across him when searching for a lost sheep.

The islanders possessed a bad reputation as pirates, but St. Columcille was not deterred from furthering the divine instructions so plainly indicated by the miraculous flight of the javelin and in due course he landed on the island. He was not received favourably. His eloquence and zeal seemed to have little effect, and finally in desperation he called on those who were in his favour to stand beside him. He eventually won the victory and was given a piece of ground on which to build his church. The first man to take his stand beside Columcille was a dark-featured man, and to him the saint gave the new name of Dhugan (the scarce dark man).

St. Columcille lived in the sixth century and the Dhugan family is still represented on the island. Few monarchs have a pedigree so illustrious or so ancient as the present head of the Dhugan family, who lives in a small humble house on this remote island.

The saint exercised his miraculous power by banishing the rats, and conferred the same power on his first convert. It is a remarkable fact that despite the numerous shipwrecks there is not a single rat on the island. I was told that a hard unbelieving man from the city of Londonderry once brought some rats, but they expired without human agency within a few minutes of their landing; and the same story is told on the island of Inishmurray, County Sligo, where St. Columcille is also credited with the banishment of the rats. And in Glencolumbkille, a wild glen in County Donegal, where the saint spent some years in retreat, the pilgrims take the clay from beneath a stone in a ruined church, locally called St. Columcille's Bed, as a specific against the rodents.

The present head of the Dugan family is a dignified old man named Anthony. Only the head of the family has 'the power,' and I know of cases where people travelled sixty miles to obtain the 'Tory clay' from him. I first heard of this clay from a postmaster in County Donegal who emphasised the fact that he was not superstitious. He had tried traps and poison to get rid of the pests, but without result, so, in desperation, he made the journey to Tory, obtained the clay, and a week after he had sprinkled it around their holes not a rat was to be seen or heard. They had vanished.

There is not the slightest suggestion of commercialism in the giving of the clay, the power being regarded as a divine gift. If one offered money it would be refused and no clay would be forthcoming. In view of the humble position of the Dugan family the temptation to exploit their reputation must be great, and it is refreshing to realise that even in the twentieth century there are ideals which money cannot corrupt. Scoffers and those who approach Anthony Dugan in a frivolous spirit will not get the clay; the gift of it is a solemn proceeding and it is never refused to those who ask for it in a reverent manner.

I was troubled with rats in my works and had made inquiries how I could obtain the clay, as I was anxious to test its power on the Dublin rats. At the door of his house I knocked and asked for Anthony. I was brought into the living-room where, seated near the fire, was an old man who told me he was Anthony Dugan. I made my request as previously instructed: 'In the name of God give me some Tory clay.'

He regarded me keenly for a few moments and then bade me be seated. Rising, he took a small paper bag from his bedroom and went out, proceeding to the ruins of a small church about fifty yards away. When he arrived at the interior of the church he knelt down and said a prayer. Then he took a couple of handfuls of clay and put them in the paper bag which he handed to me in the house. I was much impressed by the whole proceeding, which was reverent and dignified.

Unfortunately when I came home from my holidays the rats had disappeared, and when they returned after a couple of years I could not find the paper bag in which the clay was contained.

I spent some time without success in looking for a dolmen which was marked on a map of the island in my possession, and on asking two men working in the vicinity I learned the story of its disappearance. It would appear that a contractor from the mainland who was engaged in building a wall at the lighthouse cast covetous eyes on the fine stones of the dolmen. The local labourers refused to touch them and warned the foreman, who was from Londonderry, of the dire consequences that would ensue if he meddled with them. He ridiculed their superstitions and proceeded to demolish the monument with the aid of his imported workers. The horse bolted immediately the stones were placed on the cart, the vehicle was smashed to pieces, they could never again harness the horse and the man died within a year – a chapter of calamities sufficient to deter even the most sceptical from meddling with our prehistoric monuments.

Grouped around the base of a round tower in the west village are a number of antiquities, inscribed stones and portions of an ancient cross, etc., which were placed for preservation in their present position by the Board of Works. In the modern graveyard are two inscribed slabs of an early date. Some of these were recovered from the foreshore when heavy seas swept away the ancient graveyard and the celebrated cursing stone was lost.

A description of the use of cursing stones will be found in the chapter dealing with Inishmurray, where they are still to be seen. It will be sufficient to mention here that the last authenticated instance of the use of the cursing stone was on the occasion in 1884 when a gunboat, H.M.S. *Wasp*, was sent with a detachment of soldiers and police to collect rents and rates which the islanders refused to pay. The gunboat was wrecked, and all on board except six persons were drowned. Since then the islanders have paid no rates, although a nurse and a school are provided out of public funds. The islanders receive little benefit from the expenditure of rates in County Donegal. Their only road, and most of the cottages, were built by the Congested Districts Board, and it would not be fair to expect them to pay rates for the benefit of the people living on the mainland. In any event they are too poor. No bailiffs could be persuaded to make an attempt at collection, even if offered a poundage of ten shillings, and so the status quo is likely to persist.

Ruins of round tower, Tory Island.

A story is told on the mainland that a doctor refused to go to the island unless he was paid a fee of three guineas cash in advance. The islanders were angry, but as the case was very serious they managed to collect the money and the doctor went with them. But when the time came for his departure nobody would bring him back for less than five pounds, which he eventually had to pay. He arrived home a wiser, and, let us hope, a more humane man.

The most interesting of the early Christian antiquities are the round tower and the ancient 'T cross. Much nonsense has been written about the round towers of Ireland, some writers even suggesting that they are of pagan origin and have a phallic significance. They are never found except in connection with Christian establishments. We know from the records that they were used as bell towers and that they were built at the time of the Viking invasions. They served a double purpose, being also places of refuge.

The bells in use in the early Irish Church were not suspended; they were the same shape as the modern Swiss cow-bells but much larger, and were shaken by hand from the four apertures in the top storey of the tower. These apertures face the cardinal points of the compass. The single entrance is always placed at some height above the ground, access evidently being by a ladder which could be withdrawn into the interior. Before the Vikings made permanent settlements their incursions may be described as 'smash and grab raids' – they had departed with their booty before the country could be raised. When the alarm was given the members of the religious community took refuge with their sacred vessels and manuscripts in the tower, where they were comparatively safe.

The tower on Tory is built of irregular blocks of stone and is of much cruder masonry than any other round tower which I have seen; but it has lasted for about a thousand years, so the foundations must have been well and truly laid.

The 'T cross, which is six feet high, has been erected near the landing-stage. It is most interesting. Only one other cross of this type is known in Ireland. This is at Kilnaboy, County Clare, and appears to have been a termon cross marking the boundary of church lands. A T-shaped

Tau cross, Tory Island.

crosier is depicted on one of the panels of the high cross of Dysert O'Dea, County Clare, and an actual crosier of this type from County Kilkenny may be seen in the National Museum, Dublin. This shape of cross is known as the Egyptian or St. Anthony's cross, and when one finds on the high crosses of Monasterboice, County Louth, Kells, County Meath, and Castledermot and Moone, County Kildare, carvings depicting Paul (the Theban) and Anthony breaking bread in the desert, one is tempted to speculate on what were the connections between the early Coptic Church and the early Irish Church. The Celtic recluses in their isolated retreats find a parallel in the eremites of the Egyptian desert.

The Tory Island cross has three marks on it which I concluded were due to weathering, though an islander gave me another version of their origin. A wicked pagan robber, consumed with hatred of all things Christian, tried to smash it with his sword and only desisted when, on his third unsuccessful attempt, he damaged his weapon.

Lime for whitewashing and building can be obtained in districts of Southern Ireland; where the rock is unsuitable, by burning the boulders of limestone which are found in the gravel ridges called eskers. These ridges were deposited by the retreating ice sheet which had carried the stones from the central limestone districts during the last glacial epoch. In Tory no such deposits are available, so the shells of the limpets with which they feed the ducks are very carefully stored. When lime is required a hollow square of turf is built, the shells are placed inside the square and the turf is ignited and replenished as it burns away. In about two days the process is complete. Very white lime is obtained by this method.

During our stay we had beautiful weather and were happy.

When we returned to the mainland and got a newspaper-the first we had seen for many days – we learned that there had been a cloud-burst near our home in Dublin and that Britain had departed from the gold standard – at a cost to me of some hundreds of pounds.

Burning shells for lime, Tory Island.

The spinner, Tory Island.

Round coracle, River Boyne, County Louth.

An Aran currach.

Chapter Five
Island Boats

The boats of Tory are even more interesting than the farming implements. They supply the links in the evolution from the round coracle still used on the River Boyne in County Meath to the modern long currachs or canoes in general use along the west coast of Ireland. The framework of these Tory canoes was formerly made of sally (willow) rods fastened together by cords of twisted horse-hair, but the last of this type disappeared about twenty years ago. They are now made of imported oaken laths fastened to the gunwale and covered with tarred canvas. The Government supplied the islanders with large wooden boats, but as most of the fishing is with lines in the vicinity of the island the men prefer the canvas-covered type.

The Boyne coracle is probably the oldest type of boat still in use in Europe. It was originally covered with cowhide, but tarred canvas is now favoured; there is a plank seat which is placed across the diameter, and sally rods are still used for the framework. It is propelled by a paddle, not an oar, and may be seen on any day during the salmon-fishing season on the River Boyne near Drogheda, County Louth.

There is in the National Museum, Dublin, one of these coracles, covered with a hide, and an inspection of this boat inclines one to think that the round shape was due to the exigencies of the hide covering. It would be difficult to cover a long-shaped boat with hide, for several skins would be necessary, whereas one hide is sufficient for the circular boat. The round coracle is excellent for net fishing on rivers.

The popular belief that the 'dug-out' canoe (a boat fashioned out of a single tree by hollowing) is an older form than the coracle, is certainly not true in Ireland. I always

An Aran currach before covering with tarred canvas.

Dug-out canoe from a crannogue, Ballinderry, County Westmeath.

believed the coracle to be the older type, and this opinion is confirmed by Dr. A. Mahr, the Director of our National Museum in Dublin. Dug-outs are most unsuitable for sea journeys in our unsettled seas and no example has been found with an outrigger which would to a certain extent improve their seaworthiness. Numerous specimens have been found in Ireland but they are always associated with inland sites, most frequently with crannoges (Irish island lake dwellings which were inhabited over long periods right up to medieval times).

The illustration above is of a boat discovered in the course of the excavation of Ballinderry No. 2 Crannoge, County Westmeath, by the Harvard Archaeological Mission in 1933. Dr. H. O'Neill Hencken, who was in charge of this excavation, informs me that the crannoge was inhabited from about the first century BC to the tenth century AD and that as the boat was uncovered in the upper part of the crannoge it may be assigned to the early Christian period.

We are told that St. Brendan sailed the Northern seas in a boat covered with skins, and it was partly the traditions of his discoveries that led Christopher Columbus to embark on his great voyage. In the church of St. Nicholas at Galway there is a slab commemorating the fact that a Galway man sailed with Columbus. If it is true the fact is significant.

The next stage in the evolution from the round coracle is the small Tory Island canoe. The prow is blunt – only slightly pointed – there are no seats, and paddles are used. This canoe is seen in the foreground of the photograph at the top of the facing page. The ends of the gunwale project from the stern and form rests which keep the tarred canvas from rubbing on the ground when the boat is erected for carrying. It can easily be carried by

Currachs, Torry Island, the nearer boat is an earlier seatless type, with paddles; the further one is a later development with seats and oars.

Boats and currachs of earlier and later types, Tory Island.

The Rossguill Peninsula currach.

Primitive currach of the Rossguill Peninsula, County Donegal. Construction showing use of withies (willow stems).

one man. When fishing, one man sits in the stern with the line and another works the paddle, kneeling on a pad of heather in the prow.

The islanders can manipulate these boats with astonishing rapidity. On one occasion I watched the local cobbler, by name Barney Beg – i.e. Little Barney – round up his flock of ducks which had gone rather far out to sea and drive them back to land in much the same manner as a collie dog would gather together the sheep on a mountain. I was told that a mule was transported to the mainland seven miles away in one of these tiny vessels – no simple job in a canvas-covered canoe about eight feet long.

In the next stage of evolution the prow is more pointed, two seats are added, oars are used and further refinements in the form of wooden runners are placed on the bottom (see lower photograph page 35), so that the boats can be pulled upon the beach within injury to the covering. These runners were first put on about fifteen years ago.

The currachs in use on the mainland of Co. Donegal have sharply pointed prows but the stern is lower in the water than the Galway or Kerry types.

In the autumn of 1937, when on the Rosguill Peninsula in Co. Donegal, I came across one of these currachs of a very primitive type. The framework, with the exception of the gunwale, was made of hazel and sally rods, tied together with fishing cord, several of the rods forming one member in order to give extra strength.

The owner, who used this boat for lobster fishing, informed me that he built the boat himself, and grew hazel and sally bushes in order to have a supply of rods at hand for repairs.

Although they are constructed of laths and canvas the canoes of the Aran and Blasket Islands are much more seaworthy.. The prow and stern have high curves that ride the

Currachs in harbour, Blasket Island.

waves like corks and in the hands of expert men they can live through seas which would probably capsize an ordinary wooden boat. The oars have practically no blades and the island men venture out long distances into the Atlantic when fishing.

In calm weather I have seen as many as twelve people in an Aran currach. On another occasion I saw a load of one and a half tons of potatoes carried in each boat, and on the Blaskets I saw a cow transported to the mainland in one. The Blasket currachs vary slightly in size but they average about twenty-five feet in length, while the Aran currachs are only nineteen feet.

The currachs used in Clare Island, County Mayo, Inishark and Inishbofin, County Galway, have the usual cross-ribs of light laths, but in addition they are planked with thin light sheeting timber which is treated liberally with tar. Over the planks there is a layer of tarred cotton – flour bags are used for this purpose – and a final covering of tarred canvas makes a sound waterproof boat. A boat builder on Inishbofin informed me that the wooden sheeting was a great improvement because if the boat touched a rock there was less chance of a leak, whereas one had to take the greatest care when the covering was of canvas alone. The boats of Inishbofin and Inishark and Clare Island have lower sterns and are shallower than those of the Aran and Blasket Islands.

It is as easy to repair a tear in a canvas currach as it is to repair a puncture in a bicycle tyre: a piece of canvas, a needle and thread, a blunt knife and a hot turf are all the tools that are necessary. The hot turf is required for melting and the knife for spreading the tar over the new patch.

These canvas boats are not dying out. Various efforts have been made from time to time by a beneficent Government to improve the lot of the fishermen by giving them large wooden boats, but the fishermen discarded them eventually and returned to the use of the canvas boat, the reason being, as I was told everywhere on the coast, that the latter were safer in a rough sea. They are light to handle both on sea and land and· much easier and cheaper to repair in districts where there are no trees and all timber must be purchased at and transported from the nearest town on the mainland, for although quantities of timber are washed up on the islands it is generally in the form of heavy balks unsuitable for boat-building. The wooden boats disappeared from the Blasket Island about forty years ago and I do not think they will ever reappear.

I have made many journeys in these canvas boats. In calm weather their speed is incredible, and in rough seas I have never felt the slightest anxiety; the seamanship of the boatmen is superb, and never, even in the worst weather, have I been really wet. I was informed on Clare Island that in a big swell the men in the currachs do not pull hard when approaching the summit of the wave, but leave the oars in the water and practically stop pulling. If they rowed hard into the wave it would break and swamp the boat. There is no danger with the large Atlantic rollers unless they are breaking, but seas that come at right angles to the direction of the boat are more troublesome. As a large wave approaches from this direction the prow of the boat is turned to face it with a rapidity which would be quite impossible in a heavy wooden boat, and when the wave has passed the boat resumes its normal course.

As a passenger I have been fascinated in watching the manoeuvres of the boatmen. I felt as detached as if I were a spectator at a football match and somehow I had no sensation of fear although only a thin piece of canvas was between myself and the Atlantic Ocean.

Currachs loaded with export potatoes, Aran.

Currach at steamer, Aran, at the stern of the boat a horse is in the sea, the man at the back holding its head out of the water.

Carrying a currach, Tory Island.

Carrying a currach, Aran Islands.

Currachs on shore, Aran Islands.

Launching a currach, Aran Islands.

Coming ashore, Aran Islands.

Travelling to Mass by currach, Blasket Island. Note the group on the cliff top.

Chapter Six

Inishmurray, Co. Sligo

In this twentieth century it is hard to realise that within six hours of Dublin one can reach an island inhabited by more than a hundred people where there are

No Harbours	No Doctor
No Roads	No Shop
No Clergy	No Rates
No Police	No Rats
No Magistrate	No Public-house

Mrs. Waters, our hostess, had only been twice to the mainland since she was married fourteen years ago. Her household duties kept her busy. She is an excellent cook and I shall always remember the dish of lobster with sauce which was her speciality. I have eaten lobsters in first-class hotels but never have I tasted any so delicious as those on the island of Inishmurray. However, it was not lobsters that brought us to the island – it was the extraordinary collection of early Christian antiquities.

Our rest during the first night was very disturbed. There was a terrific noise, but it was merely a contest between the dogs and the asses of the island. The asses are fond of poaching on their neighbours' plots, one ass being even able to lift the latch of a gate, but the dogs guard the interests of their respective masters and chase all intruders out of their bailiwick. In several islands I have noticed how the dogs dominate the asses, the intelligence and honesty of the dog always mastering the cunning and moral perversion of the ass. There are no sheep on the island, but the dogs are useful in helping to keep the asses 'in their place.'

Inishmurray is even more desolate than Tory and is much smaller, being only about one mile long by half a mile wide. The greatest part of the surface is bare rock from which the sod has been removed for burning as fuel. It has no cliffs and the side facing the Atlantic is not higher than the side next to the mainland. So low does it lie that during the war, on a dark night, a destroyer mistook it for a German submarine and discharged a torpedo, which did no damage but terrified the inhabitants, who were awakened by the noise of the explosion.

The island was raided by the Vikings in AD 802 and also by the British military in 1921. The Vikings were looking for church treasures, but the' British military only got away with some ducks, although they ripped open the bed ticks of the islanders in their search for loot or arms. They actually had stolen a considerable amount of the islanders' property but their officers made them return it.

There are about a hundred adults and twenty children on the island. Although there is no resident priest or nurse there is a schoolmistress who takes the children every Sunday morning to a tiny stone-roofed oratory, dating from about the ninth century, where they recite the rosary.

The patron saint of the island is St. Molaise, but it is closely associated with St. Columcille. The name of St. Columba, or Columcille, signifies a Dove, or Dove of the Church, but he was not always a dove-like character; he was by birth a Prince of the O'Neill clan and the fighting instinct of his ancestors was in his blood. Early in his career he borrowed a book, a revised copy of the Gospels, from St. Finian. He promised to return it in a few days, but proceeded to copy it surreptitiously, staying up all night to do so. St.

Finian discovered him at work and demanded the copy as well as the original. The matter went to law and the verdict was, that as the calf went with the cow, so the copy must go with the original. St. Columcille refused to submit to the judgment and gathered together his adherents, with the result that a great battle ensued in which some hundreds were killed.

Overcome with remorse, St. Columcille retired to Inishmurray where he placed himself under the discipline of St. Molaise, who counselled him to go across the sea and preach the Gospel to the Picts and Scots (the latter were Irish settlers in Scotland) in expiation of his crime. St. Columcille was forty-two years of age when he founded the missionary monastery at Iona in AD 563. The sin of an Irishman was thus the immediate cause of the conversion of the Scots to Christianity.

The saint was a misogynist and in Iona he would not allow even a cow in his monastery; he said: 'Where there is a woman there must be mischief.' In Inishmurray the men and women are buried in separate graveyards. I do not know whether St. Columcille is responsible for this practice, but it certainly has persisted from early times. It is said that if a woman is buried in the men's cemetery the corpse will be ejected by supernatural agency during the night. An old woman who is not a native of the island, but 'married into it,' expressed to her son a desire to be buried beside her husband in the men's cemetery. Although he was a well-educated man he was worried about the matter and mentioned it to me, saying that he would like to please his old mother but 'doubted if it would be wise' and that he was very reluctant to make a promise that would cause him to break one of the traditions, or rather prohibitions, of the island.

Bodies cast up by the sea are not buried in the consecrated cemeteries. I was shown several of these graves, including one of a young woman around whose neck, I was told, was a necklace worth a thousand pounds! She was identified and her relations were very angry when they learned that the remains were not in consecrated ground. They bought an expensive coffin, but the natives refused to re-inter the body in their own graveyard and threatened to put it back into the sea. Eventually the empty coffin was buried in a separate grave beside the corpse.

There are no rats on the island and I was told, as on Tory Island, that once a few rats landed on the shore and died, not by human agency, before they had travelled twenty yards.

The inhabitants do not speak Irish and they use large wooden boats which entail considerable labour when they are carried up from the shore out of the reach of the winter storms. One would imagine that with the loss of the native tongue the folklore and traditions would also disappear, but such is not the case on Inishmurray. Mr. W. F. Wakeman surveyed the antiquities and recorded many of the traditions of the island in 1884, and nearly fifty years later I was able to confirm from the mouths of the people themselves the records which he had made, and heard other traditions which he did not mention. My wife gathered most of this material from the women as the men were not inclined to talk so much. The women were more communicative to one of their own sex, even though Dominick, one of the men, remarked that we must be good people because we 'brought' such good weather.

The traditions centre around the various antiquities and in no other place is there such a wealth of early Christian remains confined in such a small area. Most of the antiquities are inside a cashel, which is a circular space enclosed by a wall built of loose stones without mortar. This was undoubtedly a prehistoric fort inside which the later Christian community erected their ecclesiastical buildings, and the wall, although dilapidated, was much higher before the Board of Works 'restored' it about 1880, when they also made the present entrance and altered the position of many of the inscribed slabs. There are a couple of low entrances through which one can crawl and a built-up entrance called the Water Doon. This latter entrance is only used for the burial of those drowned, on which occasions the stones are removed for the admission of the cortège and replaced when the ceremony is over. Inside the cashel there are three churches, two beehive cells (clochans), two altars (not in churches), the Clocha-breaca, two pillar stones, two fonts and a number of inscribed slabs.

Many of the traditions connected with these remains are distinctly pagan in origin. The Clocha-breaca (speckled stones) are the celebrated cursing stones, some of which are ornamented. They are placed on the top of a rude erection of uncut slabs of rock. When a person desires to call down a malediction on one who has wronged him he turns the stones contrary to the way of the sun – i.e. right to left. If he wishes to bless he turns them left to right. (In this connection it is interesting to note that the Scots word 'widdershins,' meaning contrary to the direction of the sun, is of Scandinavian derivation.) Woe betide the party, however, who seeks the aid of the stones undeservedly or wrongly, as in such case the curse falls on the head of him who has invoked it. The rite is Eastern in origin and of immense antiquity, for in the Book of Deuteronomy we read that one altar was erected on Mount Gerizim for blessing the people and another on Mount Ebal for the promulgation of curses.

Old superstitions die hard. I have seen ordinary city people when playing cards walk around their chairs three times sunwise in order to break a spell of bad luck.

I was informed that nobody was ever able to count the stones. They always arrived at different totals, and I was warned never to interfere with the 'big stone.' Unfortunately I

Altar called Clocha-Breaca (speckled stones) with cursing stones, Inishmurray.

Cursing stones and primitive chrismatories, Inishmurray.

received this warning too late, as I had previously removed its cap for photographic purposes, but I cannot trace any misfortune due to my indiscretion, unless it be the storm during our return to the mainland.

There are two of these large stones which were apparently primitive chrismatories; each has an artificial cavity which is covered by a stone cap with a projection on its lower side that fits into the cavity and keeps the top in position. One of these chrismatories has a Greek cross inscribed on it and is certainly of very early date. In the cavity there is generally some semi-stagnant water which is used for cures. I was told that the application of this water had, to my informant's personal knowledge, cured a lump on the neck, cancer, anthrax and numerous less serious diseases. The inhabitants have no idea of its original use, but the fact that it has a cross cut on it has evidently preserved it as a holy object throughout the centuries that have passed since it was used for its original purpose. The larger stone, with which I was warned not to interfere, has no cross inscribed on it and the cavity is much smaller, but it undoubtedly served the same purpose as the inscribed stone. Although the islanders do not invest it with miraculous powers the tradition of reverence and awe still holds good after a lapse of more than a thousand years. The erect slab seen in the photograph on the previous page was placed in this position by the Board of Works. It should not be there, as the five inscribed crosses (representing the five wounds of Christ) indicate that it belongs to an altar.

The beehive cells inside the cashel are named respectively Toory Brennell, or the School House, and the Lent Trahaun, or Place of Prayer. Beehive cells are built without mortar, each layer of stones inwardly overlapping slightly the lower layer until only a

Roof formation, interior, Newgrange, County Meath.

small aperture is left at the top which is closed by a single flat stone. This method of construction is very ancient, and may be seen in perfection in the great Bronze Age tumulus of Newgrange, County Meath, which dates from about 1500 BC.

The men's cemetery is inside the cashel and in it is an interesting pillar stone, which has an inscribed cross on its west face. To this stone expectant mothers come to pray for a happy issue; they are facilitated in rising from a kneeling posture by holes cut near the edges which serve as handgrips. It seems strange that this stone should be in the men's cemetery and not near the women's church and cemetery which is situated outside and at some distance from the cashel.

Teach Molaise is a tiny stone-roofed oratory measuring internally about nine feet by eight feet. It dates probably from the ninth century and is still used as a place of prayer by the islanders. At the side of the altar stands a wooden statue which local tradition states· represents St. Molaise; it is, however, of medieval type and workmanship and one inclines to the belief that it came from one of the vessels of the Spanish Armada, many of which were wrecked on the west coast of Ireland.

Teampul Molaise is the name of another church in the enclosure. Except for its east window and the bullaun sunk in the ground at its west door it presents no features of interest.

The latest church in point of date is Teampul na Teinidh (Church of the Fire) which dates from the fourteenth or fifteenth century; and it is astonishing that a tradition which is distinctly pagan should be centred around the church which was erected last. I am inclined to the belief that this church was erected on the site of an earlier building and that the traditions of the earlier structure merged into those of the later church. The church is not orientated in the usual way, but lies approximately north and south and the altar was at the north end. It had a hearth

Stone of the Women, showing the hand-grips, Inishmurray

Teampul-na-teinidh (Church of the Fire) and Toory Brennell (School House), Inishmurray.

'The Sweat House', Inishmurray.

with miraculous powers of combustion. I was told that a man having once profaned it by a filthy act was consumed by the fire that leaped from the hearth and his charred bones are still pointed out.

Outside the cashel is a small beehive structure which is called 'The Sweat House'. This is really a primitive 'Turkish bath' and was used at one time for the cure of rheumatism and other disorders. The method was as follows: burning turf was placed inside, and when the stones forming the sides were heated the turf ashes were removed. The patient then entered by crawling through the low opening and sat on a wad of straw.

There is a great wealth of inscribed slabs dating from the very early Christian period, but as this book is not an archaeological work I will only mention one of the most interesting. I will refer any of my readers who are interested in the subject to Mr. Wakeman's detailed survey which was published by the Royal Society of Antiquaries of Ireland, but I should state that in recent years other interesting slabs have been discovered.

The slab to which I refer bears, in addition to the name, etc., of the person it commemorates, the Latin words *hic dormit.* This is the only instance in Ireland where this formula is found, although it was used in Rome during the fourth century and was common on tombs in Gaul during the fifth. The complete inscription reads: 'ŌR do muredach hu chomocain hic dormit' – 'Pray for Muredach, grandson of Chomocan (who) sleeps here'.

Wakeman states that this slab may be assigned to a date not earlier than the ninth century both from the character of the letters and because the words 'or (oit) do,' meaning 'pray for,' are not found on the earlier tomb slabs in Ireland. The crosses inscribed on the earliest slabs in Ireland are of the Greek type. I have been unable to trace any slab having a Greek cross that also bears the words 'ōr do' (pray for). The small initial cross at the beginning of the inscription is of the plain Latin type, and is additional evidence that the date of the slab is certainly not earlier, and may possibly be later, than the ninth century.

There are two holy wells on the island. One of these, which is held in great reverence by the islanders, is situated outside but close to the cashel, and is roofed over in beehive fashion. I was told that three drops of water from the well sprinkled in the sea three times each to the east, west, north and south, always produced in a legitimate emergency a calm sea on the next day. If, however, an immediate journey was necessary, three drops of water from the well sprinkled on the sea at embarking never failed to give a safe passage.

Slab with Irish and Latin inscription, Inishmurray Island.

Some worshippers were praying at the well on a New Year's Eve when they were astonished by a golden light. Most of those assembled went home with fear in their hearts, but one remained and saw Christ on the cross. I was also informed that cases of blindness were cured by bathing the eyes in the water of the well.

I found, as in most of the other islands, that the people were intensely religious. They are in daily contact with the elements, their lives are ordered by the variations of weather, wind and sea, and they feel the power of forces outside their control in a much more intimate manner than is possible in less isolated communities. These conditions of life tend to a reliance on an all-wise providence and produce a simple faith in God which is very beautiful.

I once heard a learned astronomer remark that he could not understand how any person who had studied the starry sky could be an atheist. One can get a spiritual uplift in the observation of nature which one cannot get in the artificiality of man-made cities.

In the house where we stayed family prayers were recited each night before retiring, and on Lady Day, August 15th, there were present on the island a number of pilgrims from the mainland. The islanders and the pilgrims 'did' the stations of the cross before breakfast. This entailed a walk on their bare feet completely round the island over very rough and stony ground – a distance of about three miles. In the evening a dance was held.

The time of my stay was drawing to a close and I was busy taking photographs in the cashel when I received a message that a boat would start in half an hour to take back some of the pilgrims to the mainland. The sea was very rough but we packed hurriedly and embarked, as we were told that it might be our last chance for days. I shall never forget the journey. All was well whilst the boat was in the shelter of the island, but when we reached the open sea we were exposed to large rollers sweeping in from the Atlantic. Ordinary rollers are not to be feared, but these waves were breaking at right angles to our course and were dangerous.

Most of the returning pilgrims were terrified, but our skipper, Michael Waters, was wonderful. He placed one young man to mind the mast and sail, two other men used the oars and he took charge of the helm himself. When he saw a dangerous wave approaching he shouted to the man at the mast to lower the sail while he put the rudder round and we met the wave with our bow. The boat was large and heavy and some time was required for this manoeuvre. On one of these occasions the young man at the mast was talking to a girl passenger and did not carry out his orders as promptly as he should; the result might have been disastrous, but our skipper's exhortations to his crew saved the situation.

'Will ye pull – 'tis like women ye are pulling.' 'Mind that mast and stop talking.' And to the terrified passengers, 'Will ye stay quiet?'

We got a fright which was not lessened as something went overboard, but to our relief we saw that it was only a bucket and not, as we had feared, one of the women who, in the throes of *mal de mer*, was leaning over the edge of the boat. Our skipper also was alarmed, for he ordered one of the men 'to hould that woman.' The man promptly sat in the bottom of the boat and held the woman by her legs, for she was utterly incapable of looking after herself.

We were saved by a very small margin of time, and although the manoeuvre had to be repeated on several occasions it was executed with an alacrity which meant all the difference between acute danger and comparative safety. Our crew had learned its lesson, and flirtation with the fair sex was postponed to a more suitable occasion.

We landed in the little bay at Streedagh, where only faint ripples disturbed the surface of the water and it was hard to realise that only half an hour previously we had a narrow escape from angry seas.

In the hurry of our departure I had forgotten to discharge my debt for board and lodging. When I mentioned the matter to our host he was unwilling to accept payment, but he eventually named a sum which was totally inadequate and I had some difficulty in persuading him to accept a reasonable amount. I arrived the next day in Dublin and was immersed once more in business matters. What a contrast!

Chapter Seven

Achill Island

I had often wondered what became of the old Ford cars in Ireland, as, although many are held together by wires and function long after they have passed the allotted span, they must eventually cease from their labours. The problem was solved for me as I approached Achill. They are dumped in the bogs of the west of Ireland.

The island of Achill, which is the largest off the Irish coast, is connected to the mainland by a bridge. It is thickly populated — far too thickly, for the greater portion of its surface is bog and there is not sufficient land to provide a living for its population. As in other islands, the inhabitants eke out a living by fishing but in recent years the tourist industry has developed considerably and has become an important item in the economics of the island. In addition, a large percentage of the population migrates to England for the harvest, and the money they save tides them over the winter season when no money can be earned. These harvesters are not employed directly by the English farmers, but by the firms who buy the crops, and they are shifted from place to place. They are chiefly employed in potato-digging, and numbers of girls, who are paid sixpence an hour for their work, supplement the labours of the men.

On my first visit to Achill many years ago I was on a cycle camping holiday with a friend. We had borrowed from the late R. J. Mecredy the first portable cycle tent that had arrived in Ireland. It had been invented by, and was the property of, the late Mr. Holding, on whose suggestion the C.T.C. [Cyclist's Touring Club] was founded.

We had been troubled by midges in Connemara and on arriving at Achill Sound asked an old man if the midges were bad. 'Well,' said he, 'they do be damn cross be times.' For the benefit of my readers I may mention that if one sprays one's clothes with one of the

Achill cottage thirty years ago.

modern preparations such as 'Flit' the midges will cease their attentions. At that time these were not, however, obtainable, so we thought it wiser to push on and eventually arrived at Keel.

Here we could find no sheltered spot and as it had commenced to blow hard we half-filled mackerel barrels with stones, placing them as a wind-screen around our tent, which was erected close to the shore. We slept (?) that night in our clothes.

Keel at that time was an insanitary village of thatched cottages and although we received offers of hospitality from the cottagers we preferred to chance the tent. The cottage where water was boiled for us, and where we had difficulty in refusing hospitality for the night, was typical of the island dwellings. The old man and his wife slept in a sort of box-bed inserted in the wall on the right-hand side of the fireplace in the large living room, at the end of which the live stock, cattle, etc., were housed. A glance at the sketch will convey more to the mind of my readers than is possible by a verbal description. In the room behind the fireplace the younger members of the family slept. The old man of the house told me that he was once in London, having been sent by the Government to a fishery exhibition. Unfortunately he lost his way and had great difficulty in getting to the docks. 'Sure,' he said, London is a terrible place – they are too quick for a poor Achill man. It would kill me.'

Thanks to the work of the Congested Districts Board these wretched conditions are a thing of the past, the cottagers are now housed properly and no live stock is allowed in the dwelling houses, which are clean and tidy. A transformation has been wrought in the

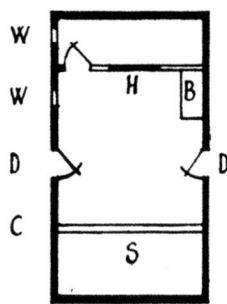

W = WINDOW   B = BED
D = DOOR   S = CATTLE ETC
H = HEARTH   C = CHANNEL IN FLOOR

Plan of an old cottage, Achill Island.

Modern cottages, Achill Island, with Slievemore Mountain in background.

last forty years which is almost incredible. Keel is now a neat picturesque village which boasts of two hotels and several houses where visitors can lodge. I have stayed several times in one of the hotels (the Amethyst). where not merely are the catering excellent and the charges moderate, but the artistic furnishings are a delight to the eye. It was originally a thatched cottage and has been evolved by the industry and genius of the local proprietors. I cannot imagine a better place for a healthy holiday.

The inhabitants are still very poor. The old age pension was a great blessing here as in the rest of Ireland, where, as some wit remarked, 'when Lloyd George introduced the pension the whole country was suddenly stricken with old age.' Many stories are told about the old age pension. There is no doubt that in some parts of Ireland there were grave abuses on both sides, by the Government and the people. In many cases the pension was not given when it was due on account of technical flaws in birth registration, which were by no means uncommon in the middle of the last century. On the other hand, I heard of a case where an inspector found that a woman who had recently given birth to her seventh child was in receipt of the pension. One inspector, a young man under thirty years of age, was told by an old woman aged seventy-five that he was a much nicer man than the last inspector.

'You must have been kissing the Blarney stone,' said the inspector.

'I was not,' said the old woman. 'I would rather kiss you.' 'Are ye married?' asked the old man of the house.

'Indeed he is not – he is too sensible,' said the old woman. Achill was, in medieval times, a penal settlement of the O'Donnel clan of Donegal; later it was under the control of the Amazon warrior, Grace O'Malley of Clare Island, and in modern times it was the scene of intensive attempts at proselytising.

I have received great kindness from many Achill people, but, as a whole, they are reserved in their manner to strangers. They will not allow themselves to be photographed although some of them will give you permission if you pay them; but generally they are averse to personal snapshots and tell you so in plain language. Once some of the islanders were on harvest work somewhere in England and saw a poster from a photograph taken in Achill. They recognised their friends in the picture, which was not happily titled, and were offended. On their return they spread the news and photographers have been taboo ever since. One girl I knew well was willing to allow herself to be photographed riding on a horse but would not consent to be photographed sitting on a donkey.

The Achill landscape is, however, the Mecca of artists, both painters and photographers. The glorious scenery of mountain, sea and cliff with their exquisite colouring forms a combination which I have never seen equalled elsewhere and which an artist told me caused him intense delight and also despair – delight at the magnificence of the colouring, and despair at his inability to record on canvas the ever changing beauty which he saw.

One American artist whom I met thought the donkeys 'cute little fellows,' and proceeded to hire one for a day to carry his easel, etc., up the mountain. He spent some hours in trying by alternate bullying and coaxing to get it out of its grazing field and finally had to give up the attempt. It was *too* 'cute'!

Achill is responsible for adding a new word – 'boycott' – to the English language. Captain Boycott lived in a lodge some distance beyond Keel. An old man told me that he was a terrible tyrant. 'Sure,' said he, 'we had to run him out of Achill and I hear they ran him out of Mayo later on.' I asked: 'In what way was he a tyrant?' 'Well,' said my informant, 'if ye spit in the yard he would fine ye. He was a terrible man.'

Keel village, Achill Island.

Stacking turf, Achill Island.

Dooagh village and Croaghaun, Achill Island.

Dugort Strand and Slievemore, Achill Island.

I was speaking one day to two Americans who were so charmed with Achill that they remained a week, although their original intention had been to stay only for a couple of days. They told me that on making inquiries in a New York tourist agency they were instructed to land at Queenstown (Cobh), spend one day in Killarney, take rail to Dublin, spend one day there, and take the next boat to Glasgow – there was nothing else to see in Ireland. Fortunately they had read some of the works of Irish authors and disregarded this advice. They travelled up the west coast and through Connemara and were astonished at the beauty of the country and the courtesy of its inhabitants.

On another occasion two English people told me that they had never heard of Achill previous to their visit. They had gone into the railway depot in Dublin and asked for a ticket to the most westerly station on the system; on arriving at Achill Sound they got into a bus which left them at Keel.

The walk along the cliffs to Achill Head cannot be surpassed; the cliffs are seven hundred feet high, and the Atlantic rollers when viewed from this height seem strangely diminutive. On the south one has a glorious panorama of the Minaun Cliffs and Clare Island, with the Mayo Mountains in the distance; on the north one is overwhelmed by the massive proximity of Croaghaun mountain, which here rises at a steep angle from the sea to a height of two thousand feet.

I was accompanied on this walk by a man from Liverpool who remarked to me that the goats made a funny noise. Thinking I had not heard him he repeated the remark, when I realised that he mistook the mountain sheep for goats. He had evidently read in a guide book that there were wild goats on Achill and thought that the animals he saw must be goats. He was a well-educated man with a nice taste in literature, who read really good books, and I could not help thinking how one-sided the life of a city dweller can be. I only hope that when the final division between goats and sheep takes place he will not make the same mistake.

Achill Head.

Harvest time in Achill Island, looking to the Minaun Cliffs from Dooagh.

Atlantic Seas, Achill Island.

Cathedral Rocks, Minaun Cliffs, Achill Island.

Keem Bay, Achill Island.

This city complex was further exemplified when a Dublin man asked me to join in a game of bridge after dinner. It was a glorious evening – the shapes and colouring of the clouds combining with the lights on the sea and cliffs to make an unforgettable feast of beauty. To stay indoors and play bridge seemed almost a sacrilege to me. I did not play.

There are many attractive places in Achill. Facing Keel are the Cathedral Rocks, where the sea has worn the cliffs into arches which resemble the architecture of a Gothic cathedral. To reach these one passes along the beautiful hard strand of Keel, more than a mile long. Walking along the strand one notices an interesting geological feature – cliffs of boulder clay, deposited by the ice during the glacial period, rise to a height of about a hundred feet. These cliffs are slowly weathering by the action of the rain, which has cut many channels in their surface and brought down enormous quantities of stones, that form a great rampart over which a road has been made that is good enough for motor traffic.

On the north of the island one must visit Dugort village and its lovely strand nestling under Slievemore mountain, two thousand two hundred feet high; and to the west Keem Bay surrounded by cliffs and remarkable for the exquisite colour of its water. Wherever one goes in Achill there are ever present the blues of the mountains and the sea, varied by the rich dull colouring of the bogs, with here and there a crofter's white cottage surrounded by the lighter greens of cultivated patches..

A short distance west of Keel there is a tiny harbour where the fishing boats take refuge, for the seas in Achill, even in the summer, can be awe-inspiring. I have watched for hours the tremendous waves which sweep into Keel Bay after a summer storm in the Atlantic. The entrance to this harbour is marked by a concrete pillar, bearing on its summit a cross. It is a beautiful idea that the symbol of the salvation of the soul of man should also be used as a beacon to guide his earthly body into the safety of the harbour.

When out here one day in a currach I caught my largest fish, a pollock of twelve pounds weight. On a subsequent visit with two friends I mentioned this fish, whereupon they immediately chartered a currach but caught nothing, and are still firmly convinced

The landmark of the cross, Keel Bay, Achill Island.

that my truthfulness was the proverbial variety associated with fishermen and golfers, although I am neither a fisherman nor a golfer. I have no time to indulge in fishing and am not old enough to take up golf, which I regard not as a game, nor even a science, but as a disease.

When in this currach we rowed through a narrow passage in the cliffs which our boatman told us was called the Dardanelles. 'I suppose it is called after the Dardanelles in Turkey,' I remarked. 'Oh, no,' said the boatman, 'the Dardanelles in Turkey is named after this.' Up Achill!! Up Achill!!

Speaking of the poorness of the soil, an old man said to me: 'Sure ye have grand land up in Dublin. I hear the sheep are as big as donkeys there.'

There is plenty of wild life in Achill. Hares abound and I saw one within twenty yards of the public road. Wild goats inhabit the rocky sides of the mountains. Otters have to be trapped because they steal the salmon out of the nets, and I once saw a fox mobbed by jackdaws who swooped so violently and cawed so vociferously at him that he thought it wiser to retreat.

Old Slievemore village is an interesting survival in Ireland of the ancient practice of summer booley migration which is still common in the Alps, where householders migrate to the uplands when the snow has melted in order to graze their animals on the higher pastures. Here the village is deserted in the winter, not by reason of snow, which seldom falls, but on account of the winter gales which rage furiously on the mountain-side. Mayo sheep-dogs are celebrated, and I saw one young dog being trained to follow his master on the public road. The man was riding a bicycle and had tied a large bone behind the saddle. The plan was effective, as the dog was never more than a few yards off.

There is not much of antiquarian interest in Achill. There are the remains of some megalithic monuments, an ancient 'Killeen' where unbaptised infants are buried, an ancient graveyard where tobacco-pipes smoked at the wake are still deposited, a holy well with the usual votive offerings, principally religious beads, and a medieval castle built by Grace O'Malley, to guard the passage of the Sound in Elizabethan times. The attractions of Achill are scenic, and to them no written description can do justice. One must see Achill to appreciate its beauty.

I cannot, however, leave Achill without mentioning Mr. and Mrs. John Barrett of Keel. John Barrett is one of the most remarkable men I know, a man of the island, though he spent some years in the USA. He has a heart of gold. If anybody is in a difficulty it is to him they go for advice. He owns the salmon fishery and is the postmaster. He is a wit with a tremendously keen sense of humour. I remember one occasion when I apologised because we were late for dinner, explaining that it took us a much longer time than we anticipated to cross a bog.

'Ah,' he said, 'them bogs is like married life.' Seeing a puzzled expression on my face, he added, 'Sure the way seems longer than it really is.'

An American was trying to pull his leg but got more than he gave and tried to find an easy retreat by asking the way to the strand. But the reply, 'When you leave the house, turn to the right and go around the fifty-second block,' left the honours of the engagement with John Barrett. I doubt if there are fifty-two houses in the whole village of Keel.

On one of my visits he discovered that I was an optician and asked me if I would test the eyes of a few old people who were unable to read and too poor to travel to a centre where they could have attention. I could not refuse such a request and made out a telegram asking for testing lenses to be sent from my establishment in Dublin. All telegrams from Achill are telephoned to the town of Westport, about forty miles away, whence they are dispatched by the ordinary telegraphic system. As the telegram contained words not in common use I stood by John Barrett whilst he telephoned it to Westport and heard the following colloquy: 'I said sphero-cylindrical. I tell ye I said sphero-cylindrical. Spell it? – Ah, that's a word ye can't pronounce, let alone spell.' Keel was 'one up' on Westport!

John Barrett and his wife have done me many kindnesses and it is with most pleasant recollections that I close the chapter dealing with Achill Island.

The Bog Road and Slievemore Mountain, Achill Island.

Cliffs, Clare Island.

Chapter Eight

Clare Island, Co. Mayo

Clare Island, which is visible from Achill, guards the entrance to Clew Bay, at the head of which is situated the important town of Westport. The mails, which are distributed from Louisburgh, are carried three times a week, weather permitting, by a contractor whose boat leaves the little pier of Roonah in the early afternoon. There is a complicated network of small roads in this district and I was astonished to see an A.A. sign-post marked 'Clare Island 3 miles' at a crossroads outside Louisburgh. I wondered if some terrestrial upheaval had taken place, as Clare Island lies about four miles off the coast. It was, however, a most useful indicator for the port of embarkation.

A farmer allowed me to leave my car in his yard, but on the arrival of the mails we found that in addition to ourselves there were seven other passengers bound for the island. This created a dilemma as the large motor-boat generally used for conveying the mails was out of action and two men had come from the island in a currach to collect them.

The sea was rough, so the boatmen would only take one very big man along with the mails on the first journey. Two American gentlemen who had booked a passage were to be carried on the second trip, so, as the wind and sea were rising, I thought it wiser to hire another boat and start as soon as possible, and it was well that I did so, for some of the passengers were not able to get across for several days.

The tide was low and the waves were breaking, but the currach was safely launched. The two men who formed the crew, myself and my son with our luggage, and another man who sat in the bow made a good load, for the sea was choppy, the wind was against us, and the currach was not a large boat. Every currach on the west coast carries inside the prow a small bottle of holy water and also, in many cases, a small medallion of St. Christopher, the patron saint of travellers. Our fellow-passenger made the sign of the cross when we started and repeated the act when we struck a bad patch on our journey.

The usual time required for the crossing is from forty-five to fifty minutes, but although our crew pulled steadily, never easing for a moment, our journey took an hour and a half. We shipped not more than a quart of water but got frequent splashings and I was glad that I wore my oldest and most disreputable overcoat, which I am not allowed to sport at home.

The approach to Clare Island is most picturesque. The island rises steeply to the Knockmore, a mountain fifteen hundred feet high which dominates a landscape that is intersected here and there by valleys and lesser hills. The grim square tower of Granuaile's Castle is on a green peninsula overlooking the harbour, near which a few small houses and one larger building, the Granuaile Hotel, are clustered together in a hollow where they are protected from the strong westerly wind.

I have mentioned on several occasions Grace O'Malley, popularly called 'Granuaile' in the west of Ireland, and as Clare Island was the headquarters of this Queen of the Isles it is fitting that in dealing with the island some account of this remarkable woman should be given.

A mural slab in the ruined abbey on the island bears the O'Malley arms and on it is inscribed the family motto, '*Terra mariq [sic] potens O'Maille*' (O'Malley powerful on land and sea'). The family motto was worthily upheld by Granuaile, of whom Sir Henry Sydney in 1576 wrote, 'O'Malley is powerful in galleys and seamen.' She was the head of the O'Malley sept and lived in the time of Queen Elizabeth. She was what modern writers

Granuaile's Castle, Clare Island

Knockmore, Clare Island.

would call 'tough' – a high-spirited, adventurous woman, who should have been born a man. She was feared by the English Government, for she held the coasts of Western Ireland and levied toll on all shipping impartially, Irish, English or foreign.

As the English Lord Deputy felt unequal to the task of subjugating her he tried conciliatory methods. Queen Elizabeth offered to make her a countess, an honour which Granuaile declined, informing the Queen that she considered herself equal to Her Majesty in every respect. Granuaile eventually went on a visit to her sister queen when her retinue created no small stir in London. The story is told that at the introduction the Queen held her hand high, but Granuaile was the taller and the Queen had to raise her hand to that of the Irishwoman. The illustration is from an old engraving which professes to show the dress and attitude of Granuaile on this historic occasion, though it was made two centuries or so later.

On her return from England her vessel was forced by stress of weather to put in at Howth, nine miles north of Dublin. Proceeding to the Castle of Howth, then, as now, held by the Norman family of St. Lawrence, she found the gate shut and was refused admittance on the plea that the family were at dinner. Incensed at such a breach of traditional Irish hospitality, she returned to her ship and found playing on the shore a young boy, the heir to the Howth titles and estates, whom she carried with her to County Mayo and released only when a solemn pledge was given that never again would the gates be shut during dinner, nor hospitality be refused to a traveller in need of refreshment. This pledge was faithfully carried out up to recent years: an extra place was always laid for dinner and the gate remained open whilst the meal was in progress.

Granuaile of Clare Island, a portrait from a late 18th century engraving.

Granuaile was twice married, but on both occasions she proved the stronger partner. Her first husband was O'Flaherty, Prince of Connemara, whose castle on an island in Lough Corrib she defended so vigorously against the Joyces that it is still called 'the Hen's Castle.' Her second husband was Sir Richard Burke, with whom she made the bargain that the marriage was to last for a year, after which either partner could dissolve the union. It was truly a marriage of convenience for Sir Richard held castles on the coast which were of importance. During the year she placed her own men in her husband's strongholds and then dismissed the unfortunate man, who thus lost both his wife and his castles.

O'Malley memorial tablet, Clare Island.

Granuaile was buried in the little abbey of the island where I was shown and handled a skull which is kept in a recess in the wall and which the islanders state is the skull of this remarkable woman.

In addition to the mural slab the small abbey contains a fine altar tomb, and the plastered ceiling of the chancel roof shows traces of paintings, among which can be distinguished a stag, a hound, another animal which looks like a dragon, a couple of faces and a harp. There are in Ireland only two other examples of medieval fresco painting – at Holy Cross Abbey, County Tipperary, and at Knockmoy Abbey, County Galway.

On the day of my visit the view from the church was wonderful. Showers were falling here and there, the sun was shining brightly, the mountains on the mainland were exceptionally clear, and the combination of land and sea with the forms and colours of the clouds made a picture of exquisite beauty. In a field outside the churchyard an old man was reaping his crop of oats; he was cutting the straw with a hand sickle and was assisted by a woman who made up the sheaves. Whilst we were watching the progress of the work a heavy shower fell and we took shelter in the porch of the modern church. When we emerged ten minutes later the sun was shining on us again, but the mountains were almost invisible, the sea had lost its colours, and suspended in the sky was a great rainbow, the brilliancy of its colours standing out in strong contrast against the background of the sky which was. now dark and threatening. These rapid changes are frequent on the west coast of Ireland and they must have an influence on the temperament of the people who dwell in these districts.

Mural paintings, the abbey, Clare Island.

The land in Clare Island is wet and boggy and, as will be seen in the illustration, even crops such as oats and barley are sown on broad ridges, between each of which there is a deep cutting for drainage. The crops when ready are carried by horses to the farmyard, and when the crop is hay one gets a weird impression of a moving haystack, as the horse is practically invisible under its load, which is secured by a rope to its body.

I never saw a cart in use. The donkeys are used for carrying turf, of which there is an abundant supply, but nearly every house also possesses a horse as the bog is some distance away and a horse can carry a bigger load than a donkey.

There are a large number of sheep, for which there is abundant grazing on the. slopes of the mountain and around the cliffs. I was surprised, however, to find geese grazing with the sheep on the mountain a couple of miles distant from the nearest house. On mentioning this to an islander he told me that the geese were all 'tokened' by holes punched in the web between the claws of the feet, so that the owners could easily identify their own birds. The geese frequently fly away in autumn and other tame birds sometimes arrive.

A stormy harvesting, Clare Island.

A mountainy farm, Clare Island.

Hares and rabbits are recent importations in the island, and I heard that, shortly after the arrival of the former, a man who had spent two days rounding up sheep and was unable to catch what he thought was one of the lambs complained bitterly when he found 'the divil was a hare.'

Seaweed is used for manure, each man having his own plot and putting out stones on the sandy portions of the shore for the cultivation of the weed. It is cut from the rocks at low tide and is made into a sort of raft which floats in to the shore on the high tide.

Seals abound here and sometimes steal the fish out of the nets, but as they have to come to the surface to eat, the men frighten them with oars and retrieve the fish. Whales, on the other hand, do no harm to the nets as they see them and swim around them, but the men fear the basking sharks, which they say chase the currachs. A man who was followed by one of these monsters once took refuge in a cave which had a shallow entrance and had to remain in it for more than an hour until the shark went away.

As in Achill, the otters are a nuisance. There are brown trout in the small lake and the rivers, but the otters, not content with a fish diet, sometimes kill the ducks on the land. The ravens are numerous and when the harvest is ripe rooks travel to the island from Murrisk, thirteen miles away on the mainland. In winter there are plenty of woodcock, and enormous numbers of wild geese frequent Cahir Island, a few miles away.

As to home industries, wool is still spun in every house but the weaving is done on the mainland. Hand querns for grinding wheat and oats were in common use up to thirty years ago, but all the flour is now imported.

'The population is about five hundred, of whom thirty-four are old age pensioners and seventy get outdoor relief, varying in amount from one shilling upwards a week. During the dreadful famine years of 1846-8 the people lived on shell-fish. Numbers perished and burials took place all over the island.

There are no police on the island, but before the Free State regime they occupied Granuaile's Castle, often having to keep their prisoners for a considerable time until it was possible to make the crossing to the mainland, for there was no magistrate on the

Transport, Clare Island.

island. The social centre is the kitchen of the hotel where, in the evening, one will always find some men sitting on forms placed against the walls.

I heard many stories of the agitation before the island was 'taken over' by the Land Commission. During the 'Land War' the entire population gathered together one evening with all the horses and donkeys on the island; they spent the night singing and dancing and turned the animals loose among the crops raised by the bailiff on a 'seized' farm. Needless to say the crops were ruined; the police were powerless, but when the excitement had somewhat died down a few of the supposed ringleaders were arrested and brought for trial to the mainland.

The country Irishman is a very astute witness in the courts and often scores at the expense of the lawyers. On this occasion the principal prisoner was asked on his oath had he not got his horse with him on the night in question. His reply, 'On my oath I never had a horse,' was greeted with cheers and laughter by the islanders who thronged the court. They saw the point which the Crown Prosecutor failed to perceive, the prisoner had no horse, but he certainly had a mare. He was acquitted.

He boasts that he has done more for his country than any of the politicians, because he was arrested later for throwing stones at the bailiff's son and spent a month in jail. He is now an old man clad in homespuns, with a white beard and of venerable appearance. Although almost eighty years of age he is out before daybreak working on his farm, and his one great regret is that he paid his land annuities when others on the island had already ceased to do so.

As we were sitting in the kitchen I asked who was the patron saint of the island. 'We have none,' said one of the wits. 'We are waiting till John O'Malley dies and then we'll see about getting him canonised.'

The Clare islanders have not lost the gift, so common at one time in Ireland, of story-telling, and they have a keen sense of humour. One man told how one day he was cutting seaweed on a rock and, happening to look up, found he was five miles out from the island. To his horror he discovered that he was moored to a whale! He did not know he was duplicating the similar old medieval legend of the Bestiaries.

Another told of a man who bought a miserable calf at a fair on the mainland, and when his friends remonstrated with him said that he had bought it because he once had a similar beast who ate all sorts of rubbish and one day it dropped a leather purse full of gold. Another man had a great idea for preventing the lobsters getting out of the 'pot' (the name given to the wicker traps used for catching them) when they had eaten the bait. He suggested putting the bait inside a glass jam jar – for, he said, the lobster would keep swimming around trying to get at it, the bait would be saved and the lobster would never leave the pot.

Stories such as these largely lose their effect when written, but when told in the warm kitchen to an appreciative audience who interject their own remarks, they add immensely to the evening's entertainment.

Occasionally a bronze implement has been discovered showing that the island was inhabited in early times, but compared with other islands it is singularly deficient in objects of archaeological interest.

Our journey to the mainland was uneventful as the sea was calm and the motor-boat was functioning again, so we only took twenty-five minutes for the passage that required an hour and a half on our outward journey in a currach.

West Village, Inishbofin, showing the Twelve Pins of Connemara in distance.

The inner harbour, Inishbofin.

Chapter Nine

Inishbofin, Co. Galway

The name Inishbofin translated into English means the Island of the White Cow. In explanation of the derivation of this name I cannot do better than quote from the *Antiquarian Handbook* published by The Royal Society of Antiquaries of Ireland, in which the late Mr. T. J. Westropp wrote as follows:

> According to native tradition Inishbofin, long years ago, was enchanted, uninhabited, and hidden in a dense mist. At last, two fishermen lost at sea in a fog touched land; they got on shore and lit a fire. Thus the spell was broken, the mist lifted and they found themselves on the shingle between the sea and a lough on the north beach. A ghostly looking old woman was driving a cow down to the lake and as it reached the water she struck it with a stick and it became a rock.
>
> The horrified fishermen, indignant at the presence of the witch, struck her; and at once became rocks which remain to prove the marvel to our incredulous age.
>
> The unknown island was accordingly called the "Isle of the White Cow."

Whilst waiting for the boat at Cleggan, our point of departure, I was astonished to hear two men, obviously foreigners, conversing in French. One of these men lives at Cleggan, which is a central depot for the lobsters that are trapped along the coast and around the islands. The lobster industry circulates amongst the islands during the season a considerable amount of ready cash, which is especially welcome since the great fall in the price of cattle and sheep and the decay of the fisheries. The principal market is Paris and the French, who have organised the industry, have agents on the different islands where the lobsters are kept in large floating hollow rafts, each holding eight hundred lobsters, from which they are transferred to a boat with a large tank.

The boat sails to St. Malo at regular intervals and carries about three thousand lobsters on each trip. To prevent the lobsters fighting and damaging each other a sinew in each claw is cut. The price paid to the fishermen is nine shillings a dozen for lobsters and eighteen shillings a dozen for crayfish. Large quantities of periwinkles and mussels are also exported. In 1934 a quota was suddenly imposed by the French Government and the Frenchman at Cleggan lost seven thousand lobsters, for which he had previously paid, before the Irish Government were able to get matters adjusted – a striking example of the folly of trade restrictions.

As we sailed down Cleggan Bay the scene was impressive. Behind us were the Twelve Pins of Connemara with their white quartzite summits, on which there was an ever-changing play of sunshine and shadow; on our right the high mass of Cleggan Head rose abruptly from the sea, its top crowned by a tall watch-tower, one of the many erected at commanding positions on the coast by the British Government. The open sea was rough, but as we approached the shelter of the island we came into calm water. The sun was low in the west, sending shafts of light through openings in the clouds, and the reflection on the calm sea of the white pillar that marked the entrance to. the harbour combined with the dark rocks to make a picture of surpassing beauty.

The patron saint of Inishbofin is St. Colman, who was a bishop at the Irish missionary settlement of Lindisfarne Island in Northumberland. He returned to Ireland in AD 667 and founded a religious establishment on the island.

An inlet, which is nearly a mile in length, provides a perfect harbour and was of great importance during the Elizabethan and Cromwellian wars. In the fifteenth century it was a resort of pirates and later Granuaile fortified it for her fleet. During the Cromwellian wars it was a place of transportation for priests and monks, and in 1653 we read that the Duke of Lorraine furnished the Irish garrison with munitions of war. The castle was captured by Cromwell, who strengthened it in 1656, and it was garrisoned by William III against French privateers.

'The inhabitants of the island to-day are a peaceful community engaged in agriculture and fishing, and I found them very friendly.

At the entrance to the harbour stands Bosco's castle. Judging by the architecture, the castle would appear to have been built in the sixteenth century with later, modifications added in the seventeenth century. Nothing is known of Bosco except that he was a Spaniard and a pirate. He protected the harbour by a chain stretched-across the entrance, and must have been a very unpleasant gentleman, for the place where the bodies of his victims were thrown into the sea is still pointed out.

Near the harbour entrance is a rock, still called the Bishop's rock. Tradition states that the Cromwellians on their capture of the castle took the refugee Bishop of Clonfert prisoner and chained him to the rock where he was slowly drowned by the rising tide. We read of precisely similar happenings in Scotland, when during the persecution of the Covenanters women were tied to stakes in a tidal river and drowned by the rising water. It seems strange that when political antagonisms are allied to religious fanaticism deeds are perpetrated which are a disgrace not merely to Christianity but even to common humanity.

There is a resident priest on the island and on Sundays it is interesting to watch the boats arrive for mass with their full complement of passengers from the west village and from the adjoining island of Inishark. The surroundings of the modern church, which is situated near the head of the harbour, are beautifully kept, and I wish one could say the same about the ruined old church still called 'the Monastery' by the

Bosco's castle and harbour entrance, Inishbofin.

islanders. This is an early medieval building situated in an ancient graveyard so encumbered with nettles and brambles that it was very difficult to get to the church. Here and there the weeds were cleared where a recent interment had taken place.

This neglect of our ancient burial places is prevalent all over Ireland, and is a disgrace to a people who profess great respect for their departed. It is apparent even in many cases where the local Boards of Health are in charge. When investigating ancient burial places I always carry a billhook and wear gumboots.

The modern interments are strangely reminiscent of prehistoric burials, several of the graves having small cairns of stones erected over them, and on others I saw round white stones and sea-shells. The cairn of the great Bronze Age tumulus of Newgrange, County Meath, which dates from about 1500 BC, was originally covered with white quartz stones that must have been transported from a considerable distance, and the Bronze Age cists of about 2000 BC nearly always contain a round white stone and frequently a shell.

At the holy well situated near the church were the usual offerings of beads and in addition some white shells. I was informed on Clare Island that the boatmen will carefully remove any white stones from the ballast and the men raised many objections when a newly arrived priest, who wanted some to beautify the church grounds, asked them to carry a supply from the mainland. 'They were too heavy' – 'The tide was against them' – and the matter was finally and definitely closed by 'Them's prohibited.'

Repairing a currach, Inishbofin.

The association of white stones and white shells with the dead has persisted in Ireland for at least four thousand years, and it is remarkable how a practice which originated in pagan prehistoric times has remained down to the present day.

The island, which supports a population of eight hundred people, is very fertile. The land is good, due, no doubt, to the deep deposit of boulder clay that covers the greater part of the island; the cattle are splendid beasts, and the life of the islanders is not such a strenuous struggle for existence as is common on most of the other islands off the west coast.

This fertility is reflected even in the bird life, which is prolific although there are practically no trees and few bushes of a moderate height. On one of my walks I observed the following: wheatear, lark, starling, wren, stonechat, house sparrow, swallow, wood pigeon, raven, chough, hoodie crow, heron, oyster catcher, ringed plover, curlew, common tern, fulmar petrel, black-headed gull, herring gull, lesser black back, guillemot, Brunick's guillemot and cormorant – a list which shows that the food provided by sea and land is abundant.

Seals are numerous. A few years ago the islanders of Inishark had a pet seal which disappeared for a few days; it arrived home at last sorely wounded, and the harpoon was identified by letters cut on it as belonging to a man in County Kerry. The nearest point of Kerry is about a hundred miles distant.

During the 'troubles' of recent years the inhabitants had no worries. The Black and Tans did not visit the island, but a gunboat once landed a party to search for arms, and they only stole one watch.

High Island, about four miles south of Inishbofin, is particularly holy. A man told me that a woman cutting seaweed on a rock was marooned there by stress of weather; she managed to climb to the island where she gave birth to a child, and was fed miraculously. As my informant stated, 'Food was there every morning for a week,' until the weather abated, and she was rescued.

We left Inishbofin a few days before the date we had originally fixed as we heard that races were to be held on the strand of Omey Island. In addition to horse races there were cycle races, running races and currach races, and it was these latter that I particularly wanted to see. But unfortunately, owing to the rough sea, they did not take place.

Omey Island is not an island at low tide, when there is a magnificent hard strand about a mile and a half long and half a mile wide, which connects it to the mainland. Sandhills overlooking the strand formed the grand stand, behind which were innumerable stalls for the sale of cakes, apples, tea and drinks. Many things divide the Irish country folk, politics, religion, social status, possession of land, but there is one great cohesive bond that unites them all – a love of sport which knows no boundary and is shared by high and low.

At Omey Island one rubbed shoulders with gentry, clergy, country shopkeepers, Civic Guards, and 'mountainy men.' Peasants in soft black hats and their wives with voluminous skirts and shawls could be seen alongside young society flappers with bobbed hair and 'lipsticked' lips. Over the entire crowd there was an air of happiness. They were out for the day – a red-letter day for the district – and even if they did lose a little money at games of chance or skill, what matter? They had for the next twelve months a topic of conversation other than the eternal price of cattle. In the horse races the jockeys were all small boys of about fourteen years of age. The admission charge was sixpence and motor-cars were half a crown, which was collected at the passage from the public road to the strand.

The poster announcing Clifden Races, a more pretentious meeting, held about seven miles from Omey Island, would surprise frequenters of Ascot. It reads as follows: 'Admission 1s., Motor-cars 2s. 6d., licensed tents £1 0s. 0d. – Roulette, thimble-riggers, etc., 3s. 6d.

'No spurs to be used and only whips supplied by the Committee allowed.'

The races on the sand, Omey Island.

The 'grand stand' at the races, Omey Island.

Dun Aengus and cliffs, Inishmore, Aran.

Chapter Ten

The Aran Islands

The Aran Islands lie across the entrance to Galway Bay and are three in number: Inishmore (the Great Island), Inishmaan (the Middle Island), and Inishere (the East Island).

Prehistoric legends tell us that Galway Bay was once a lake and that the sea broke down the land barrier of which only the Aran Islands remain. This is borne out by geological facts, for the islands are composed of carboniferous limestone which is the rock formation of that portion of County Clare, the nearest part of the mainland.

From time immemorial the islands seem to have been a place of refuge; we are told that the Firbolgs, when defeated at the battle of Moytura, fled to the islands. 'Superior' people often sneer at these ancient legends, but nearly always there is a core of truth and historical fact which modern scientific research is gradually confirming. The mythical invasions of Ireland, which were long regarded as fairy tales, have been partly confirmed by the anthropological research of Dr. Cecil Martin, published in his recent book on *Prehistoric Man in Ireland*. His research proves that different races of men inhabited Ireland at definite prehistoric periods.

On the traditional site of Moytura, near Cong, County Mayo, can be seen stone cairns and circles dating to the Bronze Age which, according to the latest opinions, came to an end in Ireland about 400 BC. When I say 'came to an end' I do not mean that the use of bronze implements suddenly ceased. The change to iron was slow, but the latter material was introduced about this date and gradually superseded bronze, especially in the fabrication of weapons. The period of bronze arrived in Ireland about 2000 BC, but bronze was a valuable material and for many centuries after its arrival flint implements were in use. A striking example of this survival is a finely worked flint implement which my son found in a pile of stones which had fallen from the wall of Dun Conor, on Inishmaan – a fort which authorities consider was erected at a time well advanced in the age of iron.

Dun Conor, Inishmaan, Aran.

The victors at the battle of Moytura were the 'De Danaan', an early race who have left their imprint on modern times. Their chief was a magical person who had three legs – a form of the Triskelion, which shares with the swastika an immense antiquity and wide distribution as a symbol. It is found on Etruscan coins, was embodied during the Middle Ages on the arms of Syracuse, and it is still the arms of the Isle of Man. The name of this chief was Manaanan. The ancient Irish called the island, which was dimly visible from their eastern shores, the Isle of Manaanan, which has been corrupted to the present title, 'Isle of Man.' He rode on the waves, whose white tops were his horses. The modern mother who tells her children to look at the 'white horses' little thinks she is perpetuating a legend that originated in the dim distant days of prehistoric times.

History always repeats itself, and we find the islands were a refuge for Catholic clergy during the Cromwellian period. The weaver at Oatquarter on Inishmore told me that his great-grandfather fled to the island from County Leitrim after the rebellion of 1798, and in our latest troubles of only twenty years ago 'wanted' men frequently took refuge there.

Christianity was introduced by St. Enda in the fifth century and the islands became celebrated as a great seat of learning and religion in the days of the early Irish Church. Their schools attracted scholars from all over Christendom and the repute of their piety was so great that the islands were called 'Aran of the Saints.'

In the present day the history of the islands is reflected by the wonderful collection of antiquities in which are represented both the prehistoric and the early Christian periods.

A steamer to the islands leaves Galway two or three times a week. The journey is about thirty miles, but the greater portion is in Galway Bay, and it is only when the Black Head in County Clare is passed that one feels the full effect of the Atlantic rollers. There is good passenger accommodation on the steamer and she generally departs punctually. This was not always the case, and I remember that many years ago, on the occasion of my first stay on Inishmore, although scheduled to sail at 5.30 am she did not leave Galway until 11.30 am. I have never been an early riser, but on this occasion I had to get up at 4.30 am and eat an indifferent breakfast, and had plenty of time in which to mourn for the hours when I might have been comfortable in my bed.

On the road to the steamer, Inishmore, Aran.

There were a few other passengers, and one of them, an Englishman, was very angry. I do not blame him for being annoyed, but he expressed his righteous wrath in an unfortunate manner. He abused everything Irish and said that the country that could not run a small steamer properly was hopelessly incapable and not fit for Home Rule. A quay labourer who was listening said, 'That is all right but for wan [one] thing.' 'And what is that?' asked the angry man. The reply, 'The manager of the company is a Scotchman,' closed the argument and was greeted with loud laughter by the small group gathered on the quay.

The steamer called first at Inishere, where there is no harbour, and we were met by several currachs which raced for the best position next to our vessel. I was an Irishman coming from the east coast, but I could not help thinking that although, geographically, I was still in Ireland, yet, to all intents and purposes, I might have been a thousand miles away from Dublin. At that time the currachs were strange to me; the men spoke Irish, they were dressed entirely in home-made clothes, woven or knitted from the wool of their own sheep, the features of the people were somewhat different from those on the mainland, and I felt that sense of wonder and interest which is common to travellers in strange places.

We disembarked at Kilronan, the chief village of the largest island, Inishmore, and proceeded towards the village of Killeany where we judged by observation, as we approached on the steamer, that we might get a suitable camping-ground. We pitched our tent near the stump of an ancient round tower in a field that gave promise of a secure hold for the guy-ropes, for we knew from experience that the wind from the west can be devastating to small tents.

We slept well and arose about 7.00 am. When we emerged from the tent we were astonished to find a number of the inhabitants grouped at a short distance in a semicircle around the tent. This occurred for several mornings and we felt bashful in carrying out our toilet to such a gallery. We could not understand the reason for this performance and it was only when we had been resident for some days that we discovered the cause. We were camping, quite unconsciously, on holy ground and the locals believed that we would be 'dead in the morning.' As we survived they concluded that we must be saints and thereafter we were welcome everywhere. This is the only occasion on which I have been mistaken for a saint, although once before, in the dusk, I was credited with being a fairy.

The islanders had never seen a tent. One man told us that he had once seen a tent at Milltown Races in County Clare, 'but,' said he, 'it wasn't a little tent like yours, it was a big tent where they sold drink.' One woman expressed her alarm and horror at gentlemen like us sleeping in such a flimsy contraption and exclaimed, 'Great God Almighty, does your mother not be afraid of your catching cold?'

On the large island there are several boarding-houses and an excellent small hotel, but on subsequent visits I stayed in one of the cottages, which are all spotlessly clean.

As on other islands, the people eke out a bare existence by fishing and agriculture, which is supplemented by remittances from relatives abroad. There is a very small margin between subsistence and actual want, so that when the fishing failed in recent years the condition of many families was pitiable. In 1933 I was told that practically every family in one of the fishing villages whose inhabitants had no land was in receipt of outdoor relief.

That such a state of affairs is possible is a disgrace to our Government, for the decay of our fisheries is entirely due to the depredations of English and foreign trawlers which commit illegalities in our Irish Free State waters that they would never attempt to perpetrate in their home seas, as these are well guarded by Government patrol vessels. They trawl well inside the three mile limit, they scoop up immature fish and, worse still, they destroy the spawn on which the future of the fisheries and the livelihood of thousands of poor cottagers depend. The Irish Free State has only one fishery steamer to patrol the coast, and the only remedy is to equip and arm with guns a number of large, fast motor-boats which should be stationed around the coast. This would be cheaper than paying outdoor relief.

The audacity of these robbers can be understood when, on one occasion, Civic Guards (Irish police) who had boarded and arrested a trawler were carried to Fleetwood as prisoners and there dumped to find their own way back to Ireland. When caught, the penalty should be confiscation of boat and gear, and imprisonment for the ship's officers. Fines are no use. One drunken skipper of a trawler boasted that he did not mind about fines, that he would make enough profit in 'one scoop of the-bay' to pay half a dozen fines. I am told that the foreign trawlers have a system of insurance against fines, so that if one of them is caught the payment of the fine is spread over a number of vessels.

The sea – without whose harvest the islanders cannot exist – is both a blessing and a curse: a blessing, because it enables them to live, and a curse, because it is the cause of many tragedies. It robs the women of their men, and hardly a family on the islands has not lost a relative by drowning or exposure. The women fear the sea and are never happy when their men are afloat; it is pitiable to see their anxiety when a fog descends on the water, for they dread the fog, which may last for weeks, even more than a storm. The islanders are such magnificent boatmen that, unless a storm is sudden and cyclonic in its nature, they can manage to win through to safety; but a fog is different – they lose all sense of direction.

Shortly before one of my visits a tragedy of this nature had occurred. A fog suddenly descended and three men who were fishing in a currach some miles out at sea were caught. They rowed for days in an unsuccessful endeavour to find land. After a week the boat was washed ashore on the coast of Connemara. Two of the occupants were dead, and the third man, more dead than alive, managed to scramble ashore, where he was put to bed in a cottage and eventually recovered. On another occasion two of the sons of the woman with whom I was lodging were missing for three days, but managed to reach the shore of County Clare, whence a telegram to the island relieved the anxiety of their relations.

The men do not fear the sea, but they respect it and will not take unnecessary risks. They know its power and their own capabilities; their whole life is spent in a constant struggle to· win a living from angry seas and bare rocks.

When visiting the large island, Inishmore, which is nine miles long and varies in width from three-quarters of a mile to about three miles, one disembarks at Kilronan, the metropolis of the islands – a village of about three hundred inhabitants with hotels, post office and several shops. Leaving Kilronan by the main road that runs the entire length of the island one soon enters a barren waste of limestone rock. The stratification is horizontal, and one sees alternately a confused jumble of weathered stones difficult to walk upon and large expanses of perfectly clean flat rock whose surface is broken by deep narrow fissures. On the surface are scattered boulders, generally of granite, and everywhere one sees evidence of the action of the ice and the later breaking up of the rock surface by the solvent action of water.

There is no granite on the islands; the boulders were carried many miles from the mainland during the last glacial period, which some geologists date approximately at

An island rockscape of fissured limestone, Aran.

Glacial boulders, Inishmore, Aran.

Making land, Inishmore, Aran

Gathering road-scrapings to make land, Aran.

12,000 BC in Ireland. The breaking up of the rock surface by solution is still in progress. Water collects in a hollow, becomes slightly acid and eats away the surrounding rock; sometimes the rock becomes a jumbled mass and in other cases a fissure is formed. From the illustrations one can form a good idea of what takes place.

Wherever soil has collected it is very shallow, but the large lime content ensures good grass, and the cattle thrive. Owing to the mildness of the climate the cattle are never, even in winter, brought indoors, and they fetch much higher prices than the beasts reared on the mainland in Connemara where the rocks are igneous and the soil peaty.

The fields, which the islanders call gardens in the English tongue, are very small and the majority of them have been manufactured. Alternate layers of sand and seaweed are placed on the bare rock, any crevices having previously been filled by broken stones to prevent the 'soil' from disappearing into them, for some of these fissures are ten feet deep; several layers, supplemented if possible by scrapings from the side of the road, form the soil in which potatoes and other crops are grown. The ridges are made with a spade and one can hear this implement striking the underlying rock when an Aran man is working in his plot. When the field is completed a wall of loose stones is built around it. There are no gate entrances to the fields.

Never take a short cut. Always travel by the small narrow lanes, called boreens in Ireland. These are wide enough for a horse or pedestrian, but too narrow in Aran for wheeled vehicles. I shall never forget a 'short cut' I once attempted. In the course of half a mile I had to cross dozens of these loose walls – no easy job, as there is always the danger of stones falling on one's feet. Even the older island men vault over them with surprising agility, but a stranger without training in the technique is sure to come to grief. When a beast is removed from a field a gap is made in the wall and rebuilt again, and, as many of the fields are some distance from a boreen, this process may have to be repeated over and over again.

An island wall, Aran.

Manufactured land, Aran

Fissures in rock, Aran.

The east sides of all the islands have lovely sandy beaches from which the land rises steeply, terminating on the west side of Inishmore in cliffs three hundred feet high. On account of this steep slope there is no water on the higher parts and curious troughs with collecting roofs have been made for saving the rain-water for the use of cattle.

The rainfall in Aran is much less than on the adjoining mainland and one can often enjoy glorious sunshine whilst watching the rain falling heavily around the Twelve Pins in Connemara. A very dry season is bad for the crops because owing to the shallow depth of soil they suffer severely from the want of moisture.

Generally the islanders can only grow enough potatoes for their own requirements but occasionally, when the summer has been wet, there is a surplus which is exported. The photograph on page 39 shows a number of currachs alongside the steamer. They are laden with potatoes which have been sold to a merchant in Galway and each currach carries the almost incredible weight of 28 cwt. in addition to the two men who form the crew.

Formerly there was great emigration to the USA, but owing to quota restrictions the number of emigrants is now much reduced and the islands are faced with an economic problem not easy to solve. Large families are reared, the islands will only support a limited population and emigration is the only possible solution of the difficulty. Cottage industries and improvement of the fisheries will ameliorate but will not solve the problem. There always has been a certain amount of emigration to Australia and Canada, but the latter country was only used as a stepping-stone for entrance into the USA

Sometimes the USA consul rejected would-be emigrants on account of faulty education. I know of one youth who 'mitched' (played truant) so frequently from school that he failed to pass the educational test, so he went to Canada, where he got some sort of a job, attended night classes there and eventually joined his relatives in Boston. The Civic Guards now see that attendance at school is regular, but the overdone Irish language policy of the Irish Government is responsible for a rising generation that is very imperfectly educated in other respects, and will in time intensify the economic problem not merely in the Aran Islands but all over Ireland.

One old islander expressed his opinion very forcibly: 'There is too much Irish, sure it is no use in America.'

The Irish language has, in other respects, been of benefit to the islands, for many of the girls obtain positions as domestic helps in different parts of Eire and during the holiday season numbers of school-teachers and Government officials stay on the islands in order to learn the language. Over the heads of all Government officials in Eire hangs the threat that if they cannot speak and write Irish within a definite period they run the risk of losing their jobs. No youth can be qualified as a solicitor until he has passed both a written and oral examination in Irish.

I have no hostility to, in fact I love the old tongue, which should not be allowed to die, but I am sure that milder methods would be wiser. In matters of this sort the motto should be *festina lente*. A partially or ill-educated, even more than a totally uneducated, population is always a source of instability and a danger to the orderly government of a nation.

The islanders are more in touch with America than with Dublin, which in their eyes is far away. As one man said: 'Sure if ye went to Dublin ye would be a gentleman.' (I disillusioned him by saying that there were many persons in Dublin who were not gentlemen.) I saw several emigrants leaving the island. It was a pathetic sight. As the steamer left the quay the last message that I heard was, 'Good-bye, Tom, and remember me to all the friends in Boston.'

Transport in Aran

Family ties are strong and beautiful, and the emigrants never forget their parents and the humble but cherished home of their childhood. At Christmas the remittances from America amount to some thousands of pounds in the large island.

The principal means of transport are horses and asses. In the large island there are many carts and a few outside cars (Irish jaunting cars), but in Inishmaan there is only one cart, which is used by the local publican for carrying barrels of porter from the boat slip, and on Inishere I did not see a single wheeled vehicle.

The horses frequently carry, in addition to the rider, a passenger who sits sideways on the rump of the animal ; sometimes a sack is thrown across the animal's back, but no saddle, halter or blinkers are used and the reins are of rope. The islanders are wonderful horsemen and it is an inspiring sight to see them, clad in their quaint costumes, galloping along the narrow roads.

Asses are numerous – practically every household owning one – and they are well treated. Between the intervals of drawing seaweed and turf, which are their principal jobs, they are turned loose amongst the sandhills where they fend for themselves. On asking a man who had some difficulty in catching his animal was he not rather a heavy burden for the beast he replied: 'Sure if ye don't give him work he gets that lively there is no standing him'.

On the occasion of my visit to Inishmaan my rest was very disturbed on the first two nights – dogs were barking and asses were galloping along the roads. It was at the time of year when the asses were free on the sandhills and during the night they quietly approached the gardens around the cottages where cabbages were grown. Listening

An old age pensioner, Aran.

Inishmaan, Aran. *"Sure if you don't give him work he gets that lively there's no standing him."*

carefully the ass would 'nose' a loose stone from the top of the wall. If there was no response from the dogs he would gradually lower the wall until he could step over it into the garden, where he made a devastating meal. The dogs were not tied up and, to their credit, this seldom occurred – they were faithful guardians but the resulting noise of battle was like Bedlam let loose.

Not knowing the cause I made inquiries and, on receiving the information, remarked that I had no idea that asses could travel so fast as the noise of their hoofs seemed to indicate. 'Well,' said my hostess, Mrs. Kate Faherty (Roger), 'do you not know that the ass travels best at night?'

I pleaded ignorance and asked the reason. The reply revealed a very beautiful tradition which I had not previously heard: 'Sure, when the Holy Family were on the. flight into Egypt they travelled with an ass by night and rested during the day, and ever since the ass travels best at night.'

It strikes one as rather peculiar on the Aran Islands and also on the Blasket Islands (County Kerry) where Irish is the vernacular that the names of the dogs should be English names such as Brownie, Dick, Beauty, etc. In only one case did I find a dog with an Irish name – 'Bran' – which was the name of Finn McCumhail's legendary wolfhound.

A heavy load in Inishmaan, Aran.

CHAPTER ELEVEN
Antiquities on the Aran Islands

The Aran Islands are a storehouse of great archaeological and antiquarian interest. The remains embrace the prehistoric, early Christian and medieval periods. Perhaps the most interesting objects are the forts which are supposed to date from about the beginning of the Christian era. They are all built of loose stones without mortar; some are circular or oval, others, known as cliff forts, are built across headlands where the steep cliffs render them secure from attack on the seaward side. The most imposing of the cliff forts is Dun Aengus on Inishmore, which has been described as 'the most magnificent barbaric monument now extant in Europe.'

Approaching from the village of Kilmurvey the ground rapidly rises, for here the island is only about three-quarters of a mile wide, and one soon arrives at the first line of defence, a wall enclosing a large area with further defences inside, the most formidable being a chevaux-de-frise about fifty feet wide formed of large stones set upright in the ground. It is no easy job to traverse this barrier even in a leisurely manner. When the attackers had passed through the *chevaux-de-frise* [defensive barrier made of spikes, or for hillforts a jumble of rocks], they had still to surmount another rampart about twelve feet high and finally the citadel wall, which is eighteen feet high. The inner faces of the walls have platforms of a lower height than the external surface on which the defenders took their stand. The illustrations show this feature plainly.

The entrances through the different defences never faced in a straight line, so that they could not be rushed, and the doorway in the last wall is less than five feet high and

The *chevaux-de-frise*, the great fort of Dun Aengus, Inishmore, Aran.

Inner wall and entrance, Dun Aengus, Inishmore, Aran.

Defences of Dun Aengus, from the citadel wall, Inishmore, Aran

only three and a half feet wide. All the defences are on rising ground, and when one takes into account the primitive methods of warfare of these early times this wonderful fort would appear to be impregnable; and it would need to be so, as there was no possibility of escape for the defenders if it were taken. A sheer cliff is its boundary and defence on the western side.

In none of these forts could I find any trace of a water supply, so they must only have been used as a place for retirement at night when the cattle could be driven inside the outer walls, or as a place of temporary refuge during a sudden raid.

On one occasion when I passed through the doorway into the central open space of the fort I was astonished to see a man fishing. He was sitting with his feet dangling over the edge of the cliff, which is undercut and at this point three hundred feet high. I went forward and lay down flat, peering over the edge, and I was puzzled to know how he could feel a bite at the end of such a long thick line that was vibrated by the wind. The explanation, 'When I do see the line moving into the rocks at the bottom I know there is a fish on it,' solved the mystery.

As he spoke the line moved rapidly and he proceeded to pull it up and landed two bream. Before I left he had half-filled the creel with large fish averaging about four pounds each.

The sinker was a large stone weighing several pounds.

When he was ready to throw out his line again he warned me and I lay flat. Whirling about fifteen feet of line around his head, the weight of the stone soon gave it an almost incredible velocity. I was fascinated, and when the line had left his hand and reached the surface of the water I was surprised to see how close it was to the rocks at the base of the cliff.

Fishing from cliff 300 feet high, Inishmore, Aran.

I offered him a fill of tobacco which he accepted and whilst filling his pipe he tied the line to one of his feet, which appeared to me a dangerous proceeding. I remarked, 'If you caught a conger eel now, he would pull you in,' to which the reply, 'He would so, sir,' seemed to partake of that spirit of fatalism so common in Ireland and exemplified in the expression 'It was to be,' commonly used after the occurrence of some calamity.

The sunsets over the sea are wonderful. If the atmosphere is clear one can watch the fiery disk of the sun disappear below the edge of the Atlantic, its progress seeming to accelerate rapidly as it approaches the horizon.

More frequently there are clouds, and through gaps in them the setting sun shoots bright shafts of light and the whole sky from south-west to north-west becomes illuminated with a brilliancy and coloured with a glorious profusion of tints to which no artist could do justice.

I have watched from these cliffs the sun setting in the west; so absorbed was I in the beauty of the scene, which lingered for some time after the sun had disappeared, that speech seemed to be a sacrilege, my pipe was allowed to go out and I was only brought to my normal senses when the chilliness of the air reminded me that I must go home whilst there was yet enough light to see my way across the rough ground. I was late for dinner, but when I stated the cause my apologies were received with a sympathy and understanding which made a deep impression on me.

In certain conditions of the atmosphere one would find it difficult to distinguish between land and sky and one can easily understand that an imaginative and romantic people would see in the mists of the Atlantic the legendary 'Island of the Blessed' which was the heaven of the ancient Irish and which they called 'Hy Brasil'. A dictionary derives the word from Low Latin, and gives the meaning as 'something of a reddish colour.' When the Portuguese navigators discovered the country of the Amazon River they recognised trees which were of a reddish colour and they called the country Brazil.

The isle of Hy Brasil is marked on Anglo-Saxon maps of the tenth century, on Spanish maps of the fourteenth and fifteenth centuries, and we even find it on maps published at the end of the sixteenth century. The similarity of this Irish tradition with the classical story of the lost land of Atlantis is remarkable.

Is it possible that in the very distant past there was high land which protruded above the Atlantic shelf, now represented by the hundred-fathom line of western Europe? The sinking of the land or disturbances of the ocean bed might have caused its disappearance, and the widespread belief and the persistence of the legends down to modern times may have had some original core of truth.

A classical friend informs me that Plato first mentioned Atlantis, and that all subsequent traditions have evolved from the story which he put into the mouth of an Egyptian priest. But may not Plato himself have merely put on record an older oral tradition? I would refer those of my readers who are interested in the subject to the paper by the late T.J. Westropp, *Brasil and the Legendary Islands of the North Atlantic... A Contribution to the Atlantis Problem*, published by the Royal Irish Academy, Dublin.

But to return to our forts: there is another cliff fort, Dhu Caher (Black Fort) also on Inishmore; it is not so impressive as Dun Aengus but it is interesting because the remains of the beehive houses (clochans) in which the inhabitants lived are still to be seen inside the protecting wall.

There are two circular forts, Dun Oghil and Dun Onaght, on Inishmore, and also two on Inishmaan – Dun Moher and Dun Conor. The latter is oval in form.

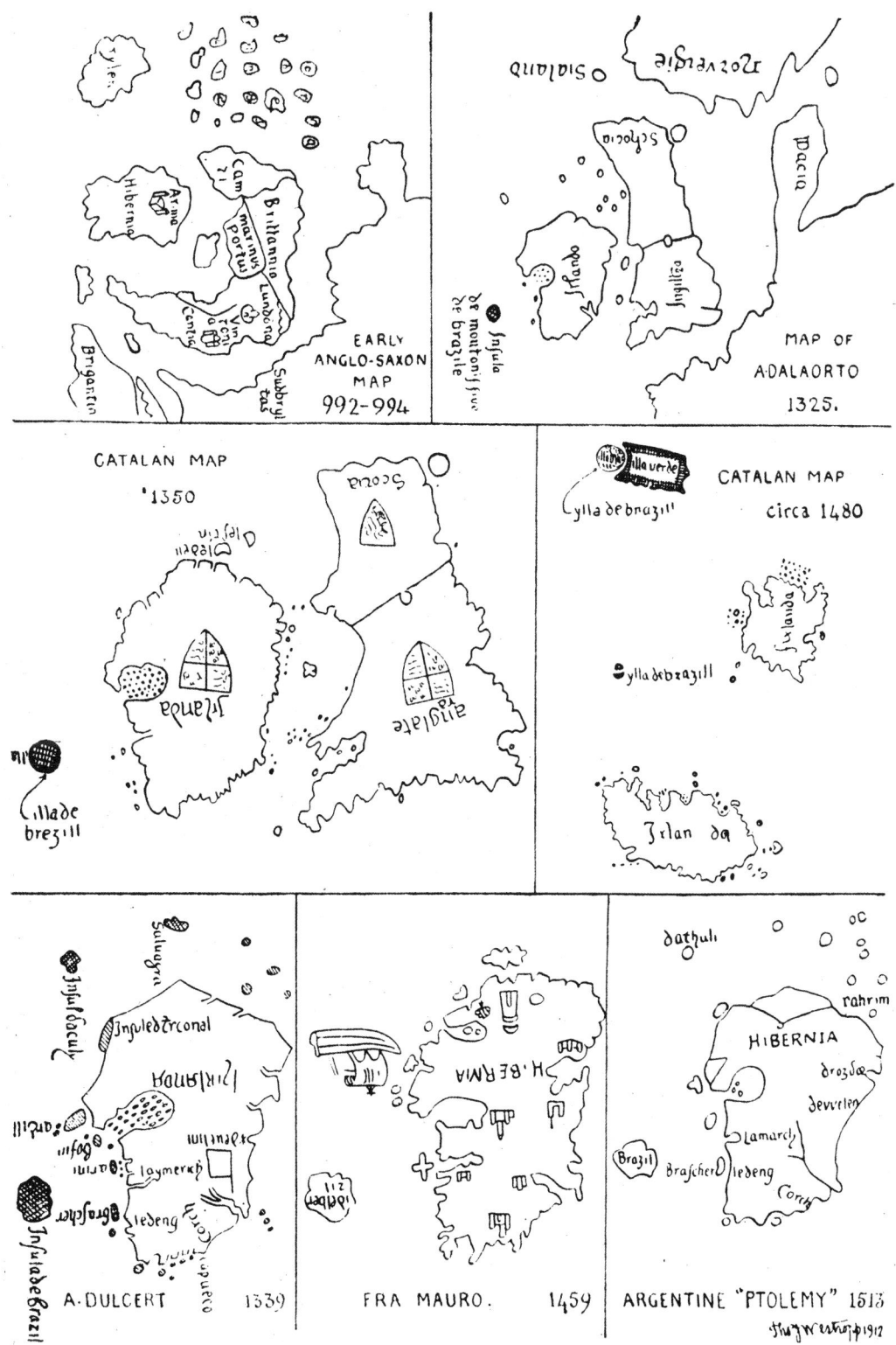

Sketches of early maps showing the position of the fabled Hy-Brasil.

On Inishere a portion of an ancient fort has been incorporated in the defences of a medieval castle. The principal entrance of the forts invariably faces the nearest landing-place on the shore.

Dun Conor on Inishmaan is from its situation, size and construction the most spectacular; it is oval in shape, more than two hundred feet long and over a hundred feet wide. Portions of the walls of dwellings are still to be seen, but these must be of a later date than the fort itself as they are rectangular in shape and our earliest stone dwellings were circular. The steps and platforms of the walls, which are common to all these forts, are well seen in Dun Conor.

Looking over the island from the wall of the fort one sees where the island men have 'manufactured' land; scattered throughout the expanse of light grey limestone rock are occasional areas of a darker colour where soil has been laid on the bare rock and crops are raised.

It was a Holy Day and there were groups of young men and women chatting together inside the fort, where they were protected from the wind – for it was early in the year – and could enjoy the sunshine. The men were delighted when I offered to take their photograph but the girls were too shy. My experience in more sophisticated communities is exactly the contrary – the women are anxious to be 'sketched' and insist on tidying themselves first, but the men are always indifferent. I found, however, when I got to know the island women and they regarded me as a friend that they were glad to be photographed, but their innate modesty rebels at the idea of 'being sketched' by a stranger. One man examined my camera and remarked: 'The man that made that made a lot of work.'

I was subjected to the usual questions that I met wherever I went in the islands: 'How d'ye like this island?' – 'Is there any strange news?' – 'Is there a war anywhere in the world now?' – followed by 'War is a great thing,' and one man said that some families who had one or two members killed had done well, as they were now getting pensions sufficient to keep them.

The men are handsome, with prominent noses, and many of them have aristocratic features. The dress is picturesque, particularly that of the older men who still cling to a tam-o'-shanter or a black hat, but unfortunately the younger generation are adopting the factory-made cap which they can buy in the shops. The black hats are also bought in the shops and an occasional jersey, shirt or pair of boots (for use only on special occasions) may also be purchased, but with these exceptions all their clothes are local products and the tweed of their coats and trousers are spun and woven on the island from the wool of their own sheep. Their clothes are heavier and they generally wear more of them than the ordinary city man – a thick shirt, a jersey, a white woollen waistcoat with sleeves, and outside these a sleeveless jacket of grey-blue tweed which is very handsome. The tweed is similar to the handsome woven cloth known as Donegal tweed, but its appearance is different, as in Aran a proportion of wool that has been dyed in indigo is mixed in the weaving with the natural coloured wool and the resultant cloth is unique and has a very pleasing appearance.

Thick, heavy, white woollen drawers are worn next the legs. They are really trousers, as they are loose fitting and are sometimes worn without the outer trousers, which latter are made of the blue-grey tweed. The outer trousers are short, barely reaching to the ankles and have a long slit which makes it easy to roll them up when the men have to wade in the sea when launching a boat.

The socks are knitted by the women and are thick and long.

Men of Aran, Inishmaan.

An Aran woman.

An Aran man.

Island footwear, pampooties, Aran.

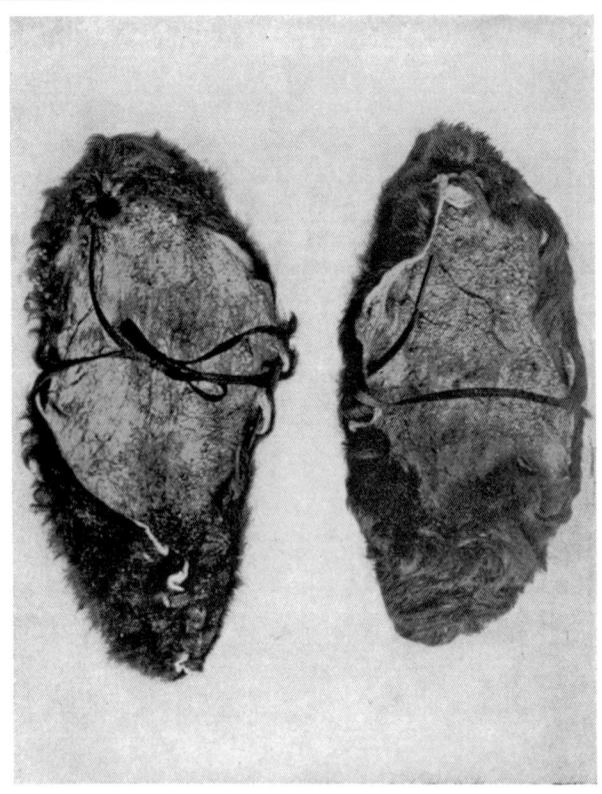

Weaving a criss (belt), Inishmaan, Aran.

They do not ordinarily wear boots, as boots are cumbersome both on the rocky pastures and in the boats. Instead they wear a sort of sandal cut out of untanned cowhide, fastened to the feet by a cord or lace. The hairy side is turned outwards and they must be kept soft by frequent immersions in water. These are called pampooties, and a pair will last for about a month when in constant use.

The wearing of pampooties, which have no heels, has imparted to the islanders a splendid carriage, for they walk on their toes in the natural manner. Even if not dressed in their home costume one can always identify an Aran man in Galway city by the dignity of his bearing, which is so different to that of the town dweller who walks on his heels.

Round his waist he wears a belt called a criss. These belts are very beautiful; they are brightly coloured and reminded me of the belts which I saw the men wearing in Provence. They are also home-made and are woven by the women by a method which is probably the most primitive in existence. It is as follows: Two of the small stools which are always to be found near the hearth are placed upside down on the floor at different sides of the room and the wool, which is of various bright colours, is stretched from the legs of one stool to the legs of the other, forming a long skein which is then removed. The woman who is weaving then places one of her feet through the skein and holds it taut, weaving the pattern by passing her hand, which she uses as a shuttle, in and out of the threads of the wool.

One end of the belt is composed of tassels which hang loose. No buckles or catches are used, and the effect of the simple pattern and bright colours is very striking.

The boys, up to about eight or nine years of age, wear a heavy skirt which I think must be a survival of the kilt, but the explanation that was given me in Connemara, where a similar custom prevails, is interesting. It would appear that the 'good people,' i.e. fairies, are envious of the beauty of human children, for their own offspring are ill-natured in countenance and temperament. Given the opportunity they will steal a human child, leaving in its place one of their own elfin offspring. For some reason that I could not fathom it is only boys that they steal – they have no use for the girls – so in order to deceive the fairies the boys wear skirts until they are old enough to take care of themselves.

Early Christian antiquities are so numerous that a detailed survey would occupy many volumes, which I fear would be dull reading for all except specialists in this subject, so I will have to limit my remarks to a few of them which are of outstanding interest.

Boys of Aran.

On Inishmore the earliest of the churches is Teampul Benen, which is typical of Irish church architecture before the introduction of the arch. It is very small, measuring internally only ten feet nine inches long by seven feet wide. The gables are high and at a very acute angle, doubtless to lessen the pressure of the outward thrust of the heavy stone roof, which has now disappeared, on the side walls which are very thick and composed of enormous stones. The entrance is narrow with sloping jambs, and although the top of the doorway is only a foot and a quarter wide the lintel is a huge stone six feet long. This remarkable building probably dates from the seventh century. Some authorities place it earlier, but it certainly is not later than the eighth century.

The very early churches in Ireland are all exceedingly small, and it is difficult to understand how they could accommodate the

Teampul Benen, Inishmore, Aran.

worshippers. When in County Kerry I noticed one Sunday that many of the worshippers had to remain outside a small modern church when divine service was in progress. They knelt on the bare ground and joined in the responses at the same time as those who were inside the building. This gave me the clue to what I think must be the explanation of these small primitive churches – the clergy alone entered the sacred edifice and the congregation remained outside.

In many parts of Ireland one finds groups of these tiny churches which are always of a very early date. When the congregations increased in numbers another small church was built and it is only when we reach the latter part of the eleventh, or the early twelfth, century that one finds churches large enough to accommodate the congregation. It was not possible before the adoption of the arch to erect large permanent buildings sufficiently strong to withstand the enormous side thrust of a heavy stone roof.

Not far from Teampul Benen is the stump of a round tower and also the shaft of what must have been a beautiful decorated early cross. Cromwell placed a garrison at Killeany and his troops demolished some of the ecclesiastical buildings, the stones of which they utilised in building a castle. The garrison was evidently overlooked, for we are told that they married island women and were absorbed into the native population.

There are many early churches, one of which bears the poetical name of 'the Church of the Four Comely Saints.' The largest group is known as 'the Seven Churches' and is about six miles north of Kilronan. The principal church in this group is Teampul Brecain. It is some centuries later than Teampul Benen and has some early features, but shows evidence of later reconstruction and alteration. In the surrounding graveyard there is a

Bed of the Holy Ghost, The Seven Churches, Inishmore, Aran.

wealth of very early inscribed grave slabs, including one with the inscription 'VII Romani' a tribute to the fame of Aran, which attracted students even from Rome itself.

After the fall of the Roman Empire the pagan hordes which swept over Europe practically extinguished learning and religion and it is well authenticated that it was the efforts of the Irish missionaries which preserved classical culture and Christianity on the Continent. These Irish missionaries founded at least seventy-five religious establishments on the Continent, reaching even as far afield as Northern Italy. The modern town of St. Gall in Switzerland takes its name from an Irish missionary and Irish manuscripts of about the ninth century can still be seen there.

At an exhibition of Italian art held by the Royal Academy in London some years ago I saw an illuminated manuscript which was labelled as coming from Northern Italy. It was not Italian art, it was distinctly Irish, and if it was not the work of an Irishman it was certainly executed by somebody who had been taught in an Irish school.

Aran occupied a prominent position amongst the Irish 'Universities' by reason of the reputation for piety of the hundreds of students who came for instruction, and it was called 'Ara of the Saints' in ancient days.

The most convenient method of photographing inscribed stones is to use a flash-light at dusk, when the daylight is strong enough to soften the shadows caused by the intensity of the flash and not bright enough to interfere otherwise with the exposure. In addition, one can place the light at the correct angle and thus save much time that would be wasted in waiting for the sun. This method I adopted at 'the Seven Churches.' After the first couple of flashes I could see that I was an object of wonder or alarm, for at every cottage door in the district there was a small group who were evidently discussing my procedure. I was, however, acquitted of any evil or satanic intent, as I had with me a well-known inhabitant whose friendship I had obtained a few days previously.

During this visit I was staying at the village of Kilmurvey, a mile and a half distant, and was surprised on my arrival home to be informed that the spell of fine weather was broken. The wind was from the east, the sky was clear, and the weather seemed settled, but my host was positive and advanced. as an argument that he had seen the northern lights that evening, and they, he said, always foretold unsettled weather. I explained that his 'northern lights' must have been my flash lights, but I could see that he was sceptical. I convinced him, however, by setting off a large flash which was so unexpected and brilliant that he got quite a shock. The weather remained fine.

Mutilated cross shaft showing the crucifixion, The Seven Churches, Inishmore, Aran

At the Seven Churches there is a small space enclosed by a low wall about eighteen inches high which is known as the 'Bed of the Holy Ghost. Here pilgrims resort. If they are suffering from any complaint the cure consists of sleeping on the bed for three Saturday nights between the Feast of St. Peter and Paul and St. McDara's Day. Blankets are borrowed from the neighbouring cottages and the cure is reputed to be efficacious.

Lying against the wall are, first, a very rude small cross, second, the damaged shaft of a cross, and, third, a peculiar-shaped stone. The cross shaft is exquisitely ornamented with interlaced ornament on one side, and the other contains in addition to ornament of a zoomorphic character what is evidently a representation of the crucifixion. The upper part of Christ's figure is missing, but the two thieves which are on a smaller scale can be plainly seen, one on either side of the central figure. So far as I am aware this is the only instance in early Irish iconography where the crucifixion is thus represented.

Unfortunately I am not an Irish speaker, but I gathered from an old man who 'had' very little English that the peculiar-shaped stone, which can be seen in the illustration, had some sort of miraculous powers and that its origin was supernatural. Comparing its shape with some of the cursing stones on the island of Inishmurray I came to the conclusion that it was originally used for the same purpose.

The people are intensely religious; they do not merely conform to the ritual of their Church but they are truly religious in the deepest meaning of the word. It is this all-pervading sense of a Divine Providence that enables them to lead happy and contented lives in circumstances that, under a materialistic philosophy, would lead to a loosening of all moral standards of conduct.

There are a couple of priests, a nurse and a doctor on Inishmore, a nurse on Inishmaan, and a priest on Inishere.

The priest on Inishere conducts mass on Inishmaan; a boat crew from Inishere brings him over and a crew from Inishmaan brings him back. It is seldom that a service is missed, as nothing but absolutely impossible seas will deter either the priest or his crew from making the journey.

It is interesting to observe the order in which the worshippers wend their homeward way after mass. First come the unattached boys and young men, then a mixed group, next after them come the young women, then the old men with, perhaps, a few of their grandchildren, and finally the old women. One of the old women shown in the photograph was nearly a hundred years of age but she walked over three miles every Sunday in going and returning from the church.

One sees, on Inishmore, many wayside monuments erected to the memory of the deceased which bear inscriptions asking those who pass by to pray for the souls of those whose names are cut on the slab. The monuments are not in graveyards but are erected close to the main road of the island where they must be seen by every traveller.

Old women coming from Mass, Inishmaan, Aran.

Wayside monuments, Inishmore, Aran.

Where we dwelt, Inishmaan, Aran.

Chapter Twelve

Music, Marriage, etc., on the Aran Islands

A portable wireless set created great interest both on Inishmore and Inishmaan. One man who had heard of it remarked, 'I hear ye have great music,' so I invited him to join the throng which gathered in Mrs. McDonagh's hospitable kitchen each evening. When the room was full other listeners could be seen outside the house where an overflow collected. At first our audience thought the wireless set was a species of gramophone and it was only when I opened the door and showed them the mechanism, and when they saw for themselves that no records were hidden in the case, that they really believed the music came from the air.

When staying at Kilmurvey, Inishmore, I lodged with Mrs. McDonagh in a two-storey house, where the kitchen contained a range and was a separate room, but on Inishmaan I lived in a thatched cottage (*facing page*) where the large living-room accommodated a much bigger audience, so large indeed that not merely was every seat occupied but every available spot on the floor had its tenant. The photograph below was taken one evening before the crowd had collected and when only a few persons were present; later on photographs were impossible.

The comments of our audience were interesting: ' 'Tis a miracle,' 'Tis one of the seven wonders of the world' – this latter expression I heard on many occasions. 'I will tell my son in America about it.' The audience especially liked to hear people talking. They knew gramophones, and music from a box was not such a novelty, but when they heard the fat stock prices they were most interested, and very disappointed when no mention was made of the price of pigs.

A small play was going on – 'Tis courtin' they are – Murteen [a youth] had better go out.'

Where we dwelt, Inishmaan, Aran.

'Tell me,' said one woman, 'how long does this be going on?' My reply: 'From about eleven o'clock in the morning until twelve o'clock at night,' brought forth: 'Glory be to God, do they never have sore throats over there?' We listened to the nightingale – 'Do ye tell me now that's the nightingale?' 'Yes,' I replied, 'and he is singing five hundred miles away in England.' 'Well, I would rather have the thrush.'

We were able to get Paris better than London, but we could not get Dublin, which was then a low-power station, although I tried several times. As the audience frequently wanted me to get Dublin I asked the reason and was told: 'Sure, we are told they are teaching Irish up in Dublin, and we want to see if they know what they are talking about there.'

These wireless evenings were very pleasant and introduced us to a number of people whom otherwise we might not have known. News travels quickly in a small community, and after the first two evenings everybody knew us and treated us as friends. We were welcomed in every cottage and the people talked freely to us.

One of our regular visitors was an old blind man named Patcheen (Little Pat) who lived in a cottage by himself. He had a little land and a cow, and neighbours helped him to milk the cow and keep his house clean. He was a grand musician and enjoyed the music so much that he wanted to reciprocate by performing the 'salmon leap,' which is a gymnastic feat that requires considerable agility, and he was very proud of the fact that he was the only man in the district who was able to do it. The performance consists in lying flat on one's back on the floor with the arms held stiffly alongside the body, not touching the ground; then with a sudden curving of the body and a tremendous muscular effort the performer stands on his feet in an erect position without bending the leg at the knees.

The old man was over seventy years of age, he was wearing heavy boots and the floor of the kitchen was smooth concrete; if he slipped a fractured skull might easily result. Nevertheless it was with great difficulty that I restrained him from making the attempt.

We made the acquaintance of Patcheen one Sunday afternoon. While walking through the village of the Seven Churches we heard music coming from a cottage, outside which was a small group of young people. We paused to watch the dancing from the doorway. The room was thronged with dancers and others who sat on forms or on the floor around the walls. Between the people we could just see the old man sitting on a sack of flour near the fireplace and playing a fiddle. Somebody must have told him that we were outside, for when the dance was ended he came towards the door and, with a beautiful dignity and courtesy, bade us welcome and brought us to a seat of honour beside himself. Whilst he was talking to us another of the party played a melodeon to which the people danced.

The old man was a great dancer and astonished us by his agility when, in response to loud requests he 'took the floor' for a jig. Every Sunday afternoon his house was thrown open to the youth of the district. They danced 'Maggie,' 'The Stack of Barley' and other jigs, reels and sets. It was delightful to see the wholesome enjoyment of those present, and I could not help contrasting the scene with a modern dance-room in any of our cities where girls with painted lips and powdered faces, and men with plastered hair, indulge in dances to the music – if it can be called music – of jazz.

There is no turf on any of the islands and this constitutes a great hardship, as it must be imported from Connemara at a cost of two pounds ten shillings for a boat-load. To eke out the fuel, brambles are gathered and cow-dung is extensively used, the droppings from the cows being put on the walls to dry and then collected in creels. The dried cow-dung burns well and gives an intense heat but the smoke is very acrid; on one occasion when the wind down the chimney blew the smoke into my eyes it caused them to weep copiously.

On my latest visit to Inishmore I went as the guest of Mr. Robert Flaherty, who was then engaged in the production of his wonderful film, *Man of Aran*. It was very enjoyable as I renewed old friendships and made new acquaintances.

Pat Mullen, who was Mr. Flaherty's chief of staff for local affairs, had spent some years in the USA, but few of the other islanders had ever previously seen the movies. One man said that he would not believe anything he saw on the screen because he once saw a man fall out of a fifth-storey window and bounce back again and 'that wasn't possible.' Another, speaking of Mr. Flaherty, said, 'I don't know where he gets all the money; ye'd think he was digging it out of the sand.'

The whole of Mr. Flaherty's establishment was invited to a wedding, and as I had never been at an Aran wedding I availed myself of the opportunity. The procession from the church was headed by several outside cars followed by a number of ponies, each of which carried two men. The cars drove at a furious pace and everybody was loudly cheering and wildly waving handkerchiefs or scarves.

The bride was a small woman who had been to America and, having saved some money, had come home for a holiday. She was dressed in a blue costume, thin stockings and light shoes; she wore a necklace, and her appearance was in strong contrast to that of the other women. It is hard to realise how she could remain contented with life in a cottage on the island, but such marriages frequently occur and always turn out well. The bridegroom was a magnificent specimen of manhood. He possessed a cottage and some land, and as the bride had some money the match was an eminently suitable one.

Match-making is undertaken on the island by friends of the families or by the parents, and hard bargains are driven before consent is given. I heard of one case where a young woman inherited a cottage and some good land from a relative. The bride was well

A bridal group, Aran.

endowed but the 'boy's' parents – all men are called boys until they are married – either had not enough cash or would not give the requisite amount. The haggling went on for a long time with no definite result. Meantime a well-to-do neighbour, seeing the hitch in the negotiations, went to Galway and sent a cable to his son in America. He was afraid to be seen sending the cable from Aran for fear the news might leak out and cause gossip. The son was home in less than three weeks, his father paid the requisite amount and the young people were married shortly afterwards.

One would imagine that marriages arranged in this fashion would not turn out well, but the fact is that one seldom hears of unhappy unions. No divorce is possible in the Irish Free State and although this has a bearing on the matter it is not the sole reason.

These simple peasants have to work hard, they accept all the responsibilities of life, and in the daily round and common task they learn a spirit of give and take which ultimately, when the children arrive, ripens into an affection which survives all their vicissitudes and binds the family life with ties which are very strong and beautiful.

But to return to our wedding party: on our way to the reception I had an interesting conversation with a fellow passenger on the car. We were talking about modern life, and my friend, an island man who had been in the USA, wound up the discussion by stating: 'The successful business man is an idiot,' and, pointing to the ground, 'the nearer a man is to that the happier he is.' These are profound truths, which in the fever of modern life are often not realised until it is too late – 'for what is a man profited if he shall gain the whole world and lose his own soul?'

When we arrived at the cottage the place was thronged; refreshments consisting of strong tea, another more potent liquid, and cake and currant bread were dispensed by the bride and groom in one of the smaller rooms. In the living room music and dancing were kept up for about five hours and then a number of the guests went to a wake which was being held in another house about a mile away.

I left early and walked home. I was afraid to wait for the car as I knew the other passengers were going to the wake, and, although I am a teetotaller, I had not the moral courage to offend the relatives by refusing the liquid refreshments which I knew would be pressed on me.

The wake lasted for two days and nights. The deceased was an old woman, and one man, describing the wake to me afterwards, said: 'They speeded her well on her journey.' Since then a 'mission' has been held on the island and spirits are absolutely forbidden at wakes. I hope the reform will last.

I was with Mr. Flaherty when he filmed the hunting of the basking shark. One shark broke the rope attached to the harpoon. The rope was at least half an inch in diameter and it snapped like a piece of thread. Eventually one of these monsters was harpooned from the pookaun (wooden boat). It was played for five hours and eventually landed on the strand at Kilmurvey. On measuring it was found to be twenty-seven feet long.

The basking shark is a true shark, but, like the whale, it feeds on small matter and is not a man-eater. It was formerly hunted for the sake of its valuable oil, which was burnt in the lamps used in the islands before the coming of mineral oil. These lamps, which are now nearly extinct, are very primitive and consist merely of a large scallop shell which sits on a small wooden bracket that was suspended from a nail in the wall. The shell was filled with fish oil in which a plaited cloth wick was immersed, the end of the wick projecting over the edge of the shell.

In recent years some of the islanders have been able to take advantage of the housing subsidy granted by the Government and have erected the two-storey slated houses which

Cottage interior, Inishere, Aran. The girl on the left is home on holiday from the mainland. The figure on the extreme right is a pedlar.

one sees here and there throughout the islands, but the majority of the population live in thatched cottages.

I have lived in both types and much prefer the old thatched cottages which are warmer and more comfortable. The living room is not so large or lofty in the modern houses and one cannot feel the same social atmosphere that one experiences when a group is gathered around the large fireplace with its open hearth and turf fire.

The cottages have two doors, one at the front and the other at the back. It depends on the direction of the wind which of these is open, but one seldom sees both doors closed. One enters directly into the living-room from the doorway. Beside the hearth there is a small recess in the wall into which brooding hens are put; behind the fireplace is another room and at the opposite end there are usually two rooms. Over these side chambers there are large lofts to which access is gained by a ladder from the living-room.

These lofts are used for storing everything from fishing nets and lines to spinning-wheels. On the walls one sees generally a small shrine with a red light burning in front of it, various religious pictures and a calendar, the latter often bearing an American address. Frequently also there are one or two large framed photographs of a bride and bridegroom sent by some of the family from the USA.

When additional accommodation is required no islander will build an extension to the west, 'for the man who builds to the west is stronger than God.' It is related that one family who defied this tradition met with dire misfortune; two of them died and another went to an asylum, so the survivors pulled down the house and built it in another place. They will actually clear away solid rock to make room for building on the east, rather than extend towards the west.

Wooden milk jug, Aran.

An Aran cradle.

In the thatch of the roof will be seen St. Brigid's crosses which are made of plaited straw or rushes and are placed there on the saint's day, thus ensuring the protection and blessing of this saint, who with St. Patrick and St. Columcille forms the most highly venerated trio of all the Irish saints.

The use of wooden utensils is dying out, but one can still see an occasional large wooden jug which is used for milk or water. Cradles are made of wickerwork and pass from mother to daughter for many generations. I had difficulty in obtaining one for our National Museum as they are objects of great sentiment, but I eventually purchased one from a widower.

Water is brought from the wells in a small barrel called a tankard, which when full is a considerable weight, and it is astonishing how the young girls and women are able to carry them. The only clear-cut division between the work of men and women is in fishing, which is exclusively the men's job, and in cooking and washing and spinning, which are the women's sphere of labour. In agricultural work, the gathering of seaweed, etc., the women share the labour equally with the men and perform tasks which would be impossible to a townswoman.

Women gather dilisk, an edible seaweed, from the rocks at low tide, carrying it in creels on their backs for as much as a couple of miles to their homes. This dilisk is sold to merchants who retail it in the towns on the mainland. I have seen it in Dublin, where amongst certain classes it is reckoned as a great corrective for a thirst on the morning after a 'heavy' night.

Women also help the men when gathering seaweed for use as manure on the land, or for burning into kelp, from which iodine is extracted. After a storm the weed which has been detached from the rocks floats in with the tide and is gathered in armfuls by men standing up to their waists in the sea and dumped on the shore. It is then put into creels which are carried on the back up to high ground out of reach of the tide, where it is spread out to dry. The weight of a creel full of wet seaweed is considerable – personally I found

Spinning, Inishmore, Aran.

it difficult to lift one – and yet girls and women perform this arduous labour working at high pressure between tides. The creel is lifted on to their backs, on which they wear a goat-skin over their clothes to protect themselves from the water. The goat-skin merely protects their back, bit their skirts, legs and feet are saturated with salt water.

On Inishere I saw men at low tide cutting the weed from rocks by means of a piece of hoop-iron fastened to the end of a spade handle. When dry it is made up into stacks which are usually slightly thatched with rushes on the top in order to prevent the rain from soaking into them and causing a deterioration of the weed.

In the early summer the dry weed is burned in long kilns formed of boulders and the result is a clinker-like hard mass called kelp. Several days and nights are required for the burning, the weed being fed slowly to the fire, which must be kept alight during the entire process. When gathering and burning the islanders work in family teams, even the children lending a hand. It is arduous and exhausting labour, and when prices are good a family will earn from ten to fifteen pounds. The kelp is sold to agents of chemical companies who pay a price that depends on the percentage of iodine found by chemical analysis.

Food – hot potatoes – was formerly brought to the workers in a conical basket called a kisaun. The kisaun was woven out of green split brambles and straw. It was an effective non-

Girls carrying seaweed, showing goatskin, Inishere, Aran.

Dry seaweed stacked for burning into kelp, Aran. Note the thatch to throw off the rain.

A load of seaweed gathered as manure, Aran.

conductor of heat, but potatoes are now replaced by home-made soda bread, and instead of milk the beverage is hot tea, sometimes carried in a Thermos flask but more frequently in a tin, which is placed in a basket and surrounded by hay. The soda bread, which is baked in a pot oven over a turf fire, is delicious. Glowing pieces of turf are placed on the lid of the pot so that the gentle heat is distributed evenly, thus producing beautifully baked bread.

I had the good luck to be staying on Inishmaan immediately previous to the great spring fair in Galway to which the islanders send their live stock. Some of the buyers came from Galway in order to forestall the fair, but the islandmen are shrewd judges, and if they are not offered what they consider to be a good price they accompany their cattle on the steamer to Galway where their beasts always command top price.

When a deadlock is reached in the bargaining a third party tries to close the deal by compromise. I remember 'listening in' to a deal which was not successful. When all efforts had failed to bridge the difference between the price demanded and the price offered by the buyer, the third party said to one of the principals: 'Ye are too hard altogether,' to which the latter replied: 'Hard! Is it me that's hard? The softest part of him is his teeth.'

The day of the shipping of the cattle is the great day of the year. All ordinary work ceases, even the children do not attend school, and for hours previous to the arrival of the steamer there is a bustle and excitement quite foreign to the usual tranquillity of the island life. Down the single road of the island come numbers of pigs and cattle. The former are generally in charge of small boys who drive them down to the slip where men are waiting who, having tied their feet together, carry them on their backs to the currachs, the whole process being accompanied by an unearthly squealing from the unfortunate pigs. When the currach is loaded it has to be rowed about a mile and a half to a position where the steamer will anchor.

Waiting for the steamer, Inishmaan, Aran.

Old woman with load, inishmaan, Aran

There is no harbour on the island and the cattle have to be shipped from a strand. I had no difficulty in finding my way, for the route was thronged with women carrying enormous loads. The creels on their backs contained, in addition to food for their husbands who were making the journey to Galway a best suit of clothes, spare socks, drawers, etc. On the top of the creels were tied sacks of wool and frequently a small hand-basket containing eggs and butter was also carried.

When I arrived on the strand the scene was extraordinary. One was reminded of the cattle hostings about which one reads in early Irish literature.

The steamer had not yet arrived and the women in their red skirts and different coloured shawls were sitting on their creels; the men were standing apart in groups, there were innumerable cattle and an occasional horse was to be seen. The whole population seemed to be gathered on the large strand, the children rejoicing in their freedom from school, and men who had no beasts to ship had come to help their neighbours to control the cattle, for sometimes, terrified by the noise and shouting, they run amuck. I was warned of the danger, and it was not an idle warning, for I saw a man thrown fifteen feet through the air by a terrified heifer.

When the steamer arrived the real work of the day began. A long rope was tied around the head of the animal and other ropes were fastened in a loop around its body. It was hustled by shouting men and barking dogs to the edge of the sea. Sometimes it refused to budge and the men had to drag or push it; terrified, it rushed wildly into the sea and was pulled into deep water by the rope fastened to its head, the end of which was held by a man in the stern of a currach. The cattle made no attempt to swim and the nostrils were kept over the water by the man in the currach, who, leaning over the stern, clasped his arms round the neck of the beast.

Shipping cattle. Draging the beast to the edge of the water, Inishmaan, Aran.

Shipping cattle. Beast rushing into the sea, Inishmaan, Aran.

Shipping cattle. Beast hoisted from sea on to steamer, Inishmaan, Aran.

On arrival at the steamer an iron hook was lowered which the man in the currach placed in the loop of the rope fastened about the body. In order to fasten the hook the man in the currach had to release his hold of the animal's head, when it invariably sinks for a few moments. This is a critical time as, if the job is bungled, the beast may drown. When the unfortunate animal is raised from the sea and dumped in the vessel, sometimes it is so exhausted that it is unable to stand, and on one occasion a bull which had struggled fiercely dropped dead.

Frequently the animal refuses-to enter the sea and lies down on the strand. When this occurs the men drag it to the edge of the water, and it invariably dashes into the water when a wave breaks over its nostrils.

The whole operation constitutes a great hardship to both men and beasts. The men do not think of themselves, but they are concerned about their cattle. As one man remarked to me, ' 'Tis a great hardship on the poor beasts, but we can't help it. What can we do? Sure we have no harbour.' The noise throughout the performance is terrific, everybody is shouting in Irish, the dogs are barking and the excitement is intense.

A fair is held in Kilronan on Inishmore, but the scenes are not so exciting, as the steamer is able to lie against the harbour wall. The pigs are lowered on to the vessel by the winch and make a great noise, but there is no trouble or hardship in the shipping of the cattle.

The chief handicrafts of the islands are: spinning and weaving, basket-making, boat-building and carpentry work.

When the sheep are shorn the women wash the fleece and put it in the sun to dry, and, in order to facilitate the drying, they tease it with their fingers. When dry it is further teased into a loose woolly mass by means of two carders which are somewhat like very large hair-brushes, having, instead of bristles, wire hooks which loosen the hairs of the wool which is now ready for spinning.

Woman and wool. Aran cottage.

The spinning-wheels in Aran are the same type as those in Connemara, but they are quite different from those used in County Donegal. The latter are more ornamental and are worked by a foot treadle which is manipulated by a woman sitting on a chair. In Aran the worker generally stands, whereas on the Blasket Islands, where the spinning-wheels are the same type as in Aran, but smaller in size, with shorter legs to the base, the operator sits down when working.

A friend of mine brought her wheel outside her cottage so that I could take a photograph, but I really wanted to get a picture which would include her husband inside the house, and to this she eventually consented. The old man had a beautiful head, his fine beard gave him the appearance that one associates with the traditional pictures of St. Peter, and, like the Apostle, his trade was that of a fisherman. Although more than seventy years of age he frequently walked to do his shopping in Kilronan, which was four miles distant. He had as grievance the fact that though he was over the age limit he was not in receipt of the old age pension. The only written record of his age was his marriage certificate which gave his age as considerably less than it really was.

He confessed to me that when he was getting married he gave a wrong age as 'he did not like to have his wife thinking that he was so old.' 'And now,' said he, 'isn't it hard on me that I am getting nothing when I should have had the pension three years ago?' To those of my readers who are unmarried the moral is obvious.

There is a tradition that the knitting which is done after dark is always the best because the sheep are asleep. There are plenty of crickets around the hearth and the islanders never molest them, for they say if you injure a cricket his friends will eat your socks in revenge.

Weaving is done by hand; the cloth wears for years and is almost impervious to rain as the natural oil of the wool has not been removed by chemical processes.

Weaving with a hand-loom, Inishmore, Aran.

Osiers are grown for basket-work, which consists of creels for carrying turf and seaweed, skibs, which are round shallow baskets used for draining the water from boiled potatoes or cabbage, and long, oval, shallow baskets called 'ribhs' which are used for carrying the baited fishing-lines.

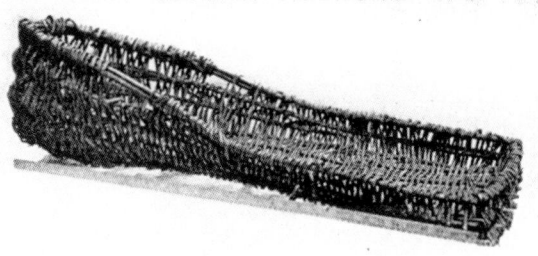

A ribh.

The carpenter on Inishere was very busy but he kindly consented to make me a couple of baskets and to allow me to take photographs during the process, for, as he remarked to my son, 'he did not like to disappoint the gentleman'; and on another occasion: 'The ould man is great for the photographing. I don't know could ye stop him if ye tried.' In making a creel the thick ends of the sally rods are stuck in the ground, the spaces being carefully measured by a straw. When watching the process I thought that this method was probably identical with that pursued by our early ancestors from whom the art has descended down to the present day. Basket-making is one of the earliest handicrafts practised by mankind.

Basket-work: making a skib (round shallow basket), initial stages of a creel in the background. Inishere, Aran

The tools used in making the framework of a currach are a plane, a saw, an auger, a hammer and a chisel. The bracket which helps to fasten the seat to the gunwale is generally a forked bough from a tree, which is much stronger than a bracket cut out of timber since the latter is liable to split on account of the grain in the wood.

There is plenty of bird life on the islands; the sea-fowl nest on the cliffs, waders on the sandy shores and larks and other small birds are numerous. One sees the chough and the sparrow hawk; swans nest on a lake on Inishere, and, strange to say, the thrushes only came to the islands about forty years ago when, driven from the mainland by an unprecedented hard and continued frost, they took refuge on the islands where the climate is milder and frosts seldom occur.

I was perplexed when I heard the cry of a curlew, evidently close at hand. Investigating, I found that a starling, perched on the gable of a cottage, was responsible. For some time he continued with his perfect imitation, which was not so loud, but identical in every other respect with the plaintive note of the curlew.

While I was loitering one day a cuckoo flew past. It was chased by a number of small birds and a man informed me that 'the cuckoo is a great lady and the small birds are her servants.' I also learned that 'if you lick a lizard's back from tail to head, your tongue will cure burns with a lick.'

Cutting seaweed, Inishere, Aran.

Woman with kelp, Inishere, Aran.

Chapter Thirteen

Inishere, Aran

The great majority of persons who go to Aran stay in Inishmaan or Inishmore and comparatively few visit Inishere, for they say that the Irish spoken there is not so pure. I am not qualified to judge the truth of this statement but it is bitterly resented by the Inishere folk, and considering the intermarriage between the islands I do not think it can be justified.

We were accorded a hearty welcome, for our hostess was a daughter of the woman with whom we stayed when visiting Inishmaan. A sheep was killed in our honour and when drained of blood it was hung from a rafter in the large room of the cottage.

Inishere does not appear to have received the attention of scholars and archaeologists that it deserves. It contains two small tumuli, a stone cairn, a large kitchen midden, several early churches and graveyards with inscribed slabs, a holy well, the remains of an early fort, a medieval castle and a later peel-tower.

I would like to do some archaeological excavation on Inishere but it would be impossible in face of public opinion, which invests these early remains with taboos which it would be dangerous to infringe. The owner of the field in which is located the stone cairn, probably a bronze age burial place, is a well-educated man who, as he informed me, was not superstitious, but he told me that his father warned him never to meddle with it because when, despite the warnings of his neighbours, he started to clear it off his land, he was seized with such violent pains that he had to desist. And another man who cleared a similar cairn from his land 'found bones and died in a year.'

In the existing cairn there is a small opening, evidently leading into the central chamber, and my informant told me that he often placed small stones in it but 'they are always cleared and the hole is there again in the morning,' the common belief being that

Our host and family

Modern graveyard above kitchen midden, Inishere, Aran.

St. Keevan's Church, Inishere, Aran.

the hole is on the path of the fairies who live in the cairn and they remove them when issuing for their nightly wanderings.

The term 'kitchen midden' was first applied to dumps of shells which were found on the Danish coast. They are the refuse heaps of the early coast-dwellers of Northern Europe and they are also to be seen along the shores of Ireland. Shellfish formed the principal food of these early settlers, but animal bones, which were split in order to extract the marrow, and charcoal are also found mixed with the enormous quantities of shells – chiefly limpet – which form these mounds. The custom of eating these shellfish is not extinct amongst the very poor. At the time of my visit one very old woman lived largely on limpets; she cut out the black portion and stewed the remainder with a little flour and pepper added.

On Inishere this midden is about fifty yards wide and a hundred and fifty yards long. The wind has covered it with drifting sand of about twenty feet in depth, but on the sides of this sandhill the midden is clearly visible.

On the summit is situated the modern cemetery of the islanders which contains layers of graves, for the sand has covered all visible traces of the earlier burials and has nearly covered the interesting church of St. Keevan which is in close proximity. Every year on June 14th the sand is cleared from the interior of the building, it is decorated with lighted candles and the islanders resort to it for prayers during the night. Many cures are reputed to take place and on one occasion a lame man was able to walk home without his crutches, which he left in the church.

The drifting sand is a source of great trouble, it has uncovered two ancient burial places and has covered several fields. We were discussing this one evening when a pedlar who had arrived from the mainland was present. He was an old Connaught Ranger who had seen service in Egypt and as a travelled man who brought news of the outside world he was welcomed in every cottage. He finished up the discussion by saying: 'Ye should see the sand in the desert,' and proceeded to paint Egypt in such lurid colours that the islanders forgot their own troubles in their contemplation of the horrors to be seen in foreign countries.

From sand the conversation veered to fishing and the depredations of the French trawlers and here again the pedlar held his audience spellbound. 'Them French are queer, I don't understand them at all. They will give good money for snails and frogs. My young fellow got a bottle of cognac for a bucketful of snails.'

'In the name of God what do they want the snails for?'

'To ate [eat], of course. But they gave him a bottle of cognac and ten francs for one and a half dozen frogs – sure I couldn't bear to look at them, much less ate them, and them all leppin' about.' He accompanied this statement with appropriate gestures of disgust and loathing. 'Aye,' said he, 'they will even give ye five francs for a rat, but it must be a house rat, not a beach or a barn rat.'

'And what do they want the rats for?' asked his horrified audience.

'To ate, of course.'

'Glory be to God! they must be queer people. And how do they ate them?'

'Sure,' said the pedlar, 'they skin them and ate them like rabbits.' Then we went to bed.

From the pedlar I bought six 'pearl' necklaces for threepence each and gave them to the little girls, the daughters of my hostess. I can still see their delight and remember thinking that the members of the feminine sex are essentially the same whether born in a castle or a cottage.

I purchased on Inishere a number of articles for the Folk Collection of our National Museum in Dublin and was informed that a German had bought 'a lot of old things' a few years previously. One of the islanders accompanied him to Galway whence he shipped

Examining the haul of fish, pedlar in foreground. Scenes on Inishere, Aran.

them direct to Hamburg. In the words of my informant: 'He had plenty of money; he took me to Galway and I pointed out a public-house to him, thinking he would stop and ask me to have a drink of porter, but it was no good. He brought me to a big hotel and paid pounds for my dinner. I would rather not have got it, because I was not up to it – would rather have had a drink of porter.'

One day seeing a man searching for something amongst the shingle on a beach and thinking he had lost something, I offered to help him, but before I had finished talking he picked up a water-worn pebble of quartz. I was even more mystified when he proceeded to split the smooth pebble into sharp fragments, and then he informed me that he wanted to cut a piece of glass. Quartz is next to the gems in the scale of hardness and is nearly as efficient as the diamond which is commonly used for this purpose by glass merchants.

We were awakened each morning by our host who announced the arrival of my shaving water by, 'There's water here to scald ye.' When dinner was ready our hostess would say: 'Let ye come in now.'

I shall never forget the pleasant times I have had in the society of my Aran friends. I remember the hospitality I received in their homes. 'Ye are welcome,' and when I rose to go, 'Let ye come again.' I remember the talks around the fireside during the evenings.

It was always with feelings of regret that I returned from these quiet islands to the life that awaited me in the city of Dublin, but I always came back renewed in body and spirit and with a more philosophic outlook on the worries and distractions of modern business, for in Aran one sees that the real wants of humanity are few and one realises that the eternal verities are more essential to happiness than the feverish pursuit of wealth or fame or amusement which absorbs the energies and the minds of so many misguided people in this twentieth century.

The steamer had blown her siren, the currach was waiting, so I said good-bye to my many friends and embarked. The last words that I heard were, 'God speed ye – I wish ye a safe journey.'

Chapter Fourteen

The Blasket Islands
(The next Parish to America)

The Blasket Islands. are situated off the coast of the peninsula of Corcaguiney, County Kerry, a large peninsula, thirty miles in length, containing some of the highest mountains in Ireland and one town, Dingle, which supplies the wants of a large area. The islands are a continuation of the mountain range of the mainland and rise in places to a height of nearly a thousand feet.

There is no church or shop and, whilst the hardships of life on the sea are just as severe as on the Aran Islands, yet one feels that the struggle for a subsistence is not so hard. The topography of the islands, with their ample supply of turf for fuel and plenteous grazing for the sheep, is in striking contrast to the low altitude and barren rocky pastures of many of the islands off the coast of County Galway. There are a number of islands, but the largest, the Great Blasket, is the only one that is permanently inhabited; the others are used for grazing purposes during the summer months and are occasionally occupied for a few days in the lobster-fishing season.

We had arranged to cross from the mainland with Dr. Flower of the British Museum. He had frequently visited the island and we are indebted to him for our introductions to the islanders. As friends of his we were immediately welcomed, and we were not treated as strangers.

We set out in two currachs from a sheltered cove at Dunquin, but when we got into the Sound the sea and the wind were contrary, so we ran for the shelter of the small island of Beginish whence we had a calmer passage to the Blasket. The direct passage across the Sound is only about three miles but we must have covered seven or eight miles in our journey.

The sea was sufficiently rough to give one a slight thrill, without any sense of real danger. One of the boats hoisted a sail; just at the moment when the sail was up and the men had ceased rowing the currach remained stationary, poised on a large wave. Our

South side of Great Blasket Island.

boat, close by, was in the trough of the sea and, looking upwards, we could see the other currach suspended as it were by invisible wires. My camera lay open on my knees, but I was so entranced by the unique beauty of the sight that I never thought of using it. When I came to my senses it was too late. I have ever since regretted this lost opportunity; but are not our lives compounded largely of lost opportunities? Too often we fail to grasp the beautiful things of life – the occasion to do a kindly act, or to give utterance to a friendly thought; we remember when it is too late, and the opportunity may never occur again.

A visitor told me of a rather terrifying experience that he had on one of his numerous crossings. It was a bad evening, the sea was very rough and visibility was reduced to a very limited distance by sheets of misty rain driven by a strong wind. The boatmen who met him at Dunquin had not expressed any doubts about the wisdom of crossing and as they are splendid seamen no thought of danger entered his mind when he saw his wife and family embark.

He watched the progress of the currach till in a minute or two it was lost from sight in the mist, and then turned to the crew who were to carry himself and the luggage. To his astonishment and horror they refused to embark. 'Why,' he asked, 'did you let my family go if the crossing is not safe?? 'It is safe enough in their canoe, but ours is not such a good boat and we will not go.' There was nothing to be done, so he had to stay on the mainland, a prey to anxiety. Luckily the next morning was fine and he had arrived on the Blasket before his wife had learned of his absence, for she had been in a state of collapse and was put to bed immediately on her arrival on the previous evening.

Communication with the mainland is often impossible for weeks as the small harbour at Dunquin is exposed to the south-westerly gales, and on the island the harbour (?) is a tiny creek between rocks which have been connected by a cement wall. In a rough sea it is extremely difficult to make an entry through the narrow entrance channel. Frequently in the winter supplies of tea or flour run short, but when this occurs the islanders who have lend to those who have not, until a journey to the mainland is possible.

On our arrival Dr. Flower was enthusiastically welcomed for he was an old friend and they never called him by his name – to them he was 'Blaheen,' a name of affection which; translated into English, means 'Little Flower.'

My hostess was Mrs. Keane (Buffer); the affix is to distinguish her from others of the same name, for Keane is the principal name on the island. The King of the Island is always a member of the Keane family. When I was there the chief man was a fine specimen of manhood who in addition to his ordinary pursuits acted as postman, travelling to the mainland

Our hostess and daughter, Mrs Keane (Buffer).

North side, Great Blasket Island.

The village from the Blasket Sound, Great Blasket Island.

Sunset over the Blasket Islands.

Cottages, Great Blasket Island.

The Path of the Galleon, *Our Lady of the Rosary*, Great Blasket Village with Begnish on right.

two or three times a week, weather permitting, to collect the mails. There was no necessity to deliver the letters for he was always met on arrival by a number of the islanders.

It was interesting to note that the vast majority of the letters bore USA stamps for, as I found in other islands, there was formerly great emigration to America. My hostess had four daughters and two sons in Hartford, Connecticut, and one daughter in London. Only one daughter and one son remained at home, and since we were there the daughter has married on the mainland. The daughter was extraordinarily bright and attractive and the mother had a sweet face that was the true index of a beautiful character.

The village is on the east side of the island facing the mainland. The cottages have rather a peculiar appearance as the roofs are all covered with tarred felt, which contrasts strongly with the whitewashed walls. They are arranged in rows having their ends towards the sea with the gable of the highest cottage in many cases touching the solid rock. The hill is fairly steep so that when one walks on the main road the chimneys are frequently on a level with one's head. Santa Claus would have no difficult job on the Blaskets.

Formerly the cottages were thatched with rushes and, owing to the easy access to the roofs, the hens often nested there. The children had to retrieve the eggs and much damage occurred in the process. I heard a story of one man who had found a newly fledged chicken in his porridge. But the limit was surely reached when a simpleton came through a roof and, on being asked what he was doing, explained that he was looking for his mother's cow.

The interiors of the cottages also are different from those in Aran. The fireplace is small and projects into the living room, and it lacks the ingle walls which make such cosy corners. These features can be plainly seen in the photograph below. Hanging on the walls are the usual religious pictures and, occasionally, pictures of the national heroes of Ireland, ranging from Brian Boru to Patrick Pearse. In the few two-storey slated houses built by the Government the large fireplaces have been built up.

Interior of cottage, Blasket Island.

Before taking a flash-light photograph of the interior of one of the cottages I thought it wise to warn my victims about the bright flash, and demonstrated it by throwing a small charge on to the glowing fire. Even though warned, the woman of the house was startled, much to the amusement of her husband who seemed to be delighted at this exhibition of feminine weakness. He had a twinkle in his eye as he remarked: 'Ye are a great man. When will ye come again to this island?'

In another cottage I set off the flash just inside the open doorway so that it was seen from other houses and the islanders, thinking a thunderbolt had fallen, sprinkled holy water around their homesteads. We had thunder a couple of days later, when I noticed that holy water was again used. The old woman whose cottage I had photographed was sure her house had been burnt down. After the flash, when she was again able to see clearly, she remarked to me: 'I hoped you would burn the house down, for then I would get great insurance.'

The view from the cottage in which we lodged was superb. Across the narrow sound was Mount Eagle, its southern extremity ending abruptly in Slea Head. To the north were Sybil Head and the Three Sisters, headlands with cliffs hundreds of feet high and guarding the entrance to Smerwick Harbour, the scene of the massacre so graphically described in Kingsley's novel, *Westward Ho!*, when the Lord Deputy Grey, assisted by Sir Walter Raleigh, butchered in cold blood about six hundred Spanish and Italian prisoners in 1580. In the distance can be seen Mount Brandon, the second highest mountain in Ireland, its summit usually lost in mist and cloud.

In the evening we frequently went to the northern point of the island about a mile from the village to gaze over the evening sky, which the setting sun invested with glorious colours. At the time of our visit in the month of June the sun set behind the island of Inishtooskert, which appeared like some reptilian monster, dark and threatening, with its jagged profile silhouetted against the sky and its body in shadow, straddling across the ocean. At this point also is the only flat piece of land, where in summer evenings the younger boys play football and the older lads and the girls dance to the music of melodeon or fiddle. On wet Sunday evenings they adjourn to Old Peg's House, which is locally called 'The Dail' or talking place.

Boy with Turf, Blasket Island.

One evening during my stay, after a day of very heavy and continuous rain, I tried to use my portable wireless set but unfortunately something had gone wrong and the only item I was able to get was the weather report, which stated: 'It has been raining in the west of Ireland,' much to the amusement of my audience, who were well aware of the fact. This announcement was followed by 'God Save the King' played by a band. As the walls of the cottage were decorated with pictures of the leaders of the 1916 insurrection I was uneasy in my mind. Luckily, however, the islanders did not know the tune and the situation was saved.

Primroses grow in great profusion, the flowers being exceptionally large owing to the soft, moist climate, and that favourite plant of suburban gardens, 'London pride,' also grows wild. In front of some of the cottages flowers are grown and arum lilies thrive in the open air. An English visitor once sent as a present some packets of small seedlings which were duly planted and in course of time produced a crop of 'London pride,' much to the disappointment of the islanders who regard this plant as an unattractive weed.

Many of the ships of the Spanish Armada were wrecked on the west coast of Ireland in 1588. At least one ship, *Our Lady of the Rosary*, a magnificent vessel of a thousand tons, was wrecked in the Blasket Sound, and among the many who perished was an illegitimate son of King Philip of Spain, who was buried in the old graveyard of Vicarstown on the mainland. All that remains to show the last resting-place of this proud Spaniard is a plain stone, without an inscription, in a small neglected cemetery overgrown with bracken on the slopes of a mountain in Kerry – '*sic transit gloria mundi.*'

It is almost three hundred and fifty years since the Spanish Armada set sail, and when I was on the Blasket Island I heard from Dr. Flower the story of this wreck*.

The wind was blowing from the north-west and *Our Lady of the Rosary*, by a feat of wonderful seamanship or almost incredible good fortune, safely threaded her way between the innumerable rocks and through the narrow channel that separates the small island of Beginish from the Blasket. Arrived safely in the Sound, she cast anchor opposite the modern village, where she was protected from the north-west gale. During the night the wind increased to a hurricane and shifted to the south, to which quarter *Our Lady of the Rosary* was exposed without any protection. It was impossible to manoeuvre in the narrow channel – the vessel dragged her anchors and was dashed to pieces on the terrible cliffs of the mainland.

Sic transit gloria mundi: The grave of an Armada Spanish Prince, Vicarstown, County Kerry.

---

* Publisher's note: Dr. Flower was mistaken as to the identity of the ship. It was the *Santa Maria de la Rosa* that suffered the fate described above on 21st September 1588, and reputedly had among her complement a Spanish Prince. A false claim but valuable propaganda for the English. The wreck was located in 1968 in about 30 metres of water. Many cannonballs were found, but the ship's castle containing the guns was not. *Nuestra Señora del Rosario* (*Our lady of the Rosary*) was also an Armada ship, but was captured in the English Channel by the English ship *Revenge* on the 1st August 1588.

Much flotsam and jetsam is thrown up by the sea. During the war the islanders were well off, for in addition to getting high prices for their sheep and wool, they obtained a lot of wreckage. Old electric bulbs are popular ornaments, ship's buckets and masts can be seen, and much of the furniture is made from ship's fittings.

There is, or rather was, for it is dead, only one small tree on the island. It stands outside one of the new houses and is used for drying clothes.

The men wear the ordinary clothes of fishermen, and in the case of the younger men a cap is worn, but the headgear of the older men is usually a black soft hat with a broad brim. They shave once a week. The women wear voluminous skirts and shawls; in the house a small shawl is worn over the head, but when out of doors a heavy shawl covers shoulders and head. The younger women are departing from the old heavy type of dress, and the illustration of our hostess and her daughter shows the great contrast.

My wife was talking to a good-looking, beautifully built, slender young woman, aged twenty-three, when a very stout woman came into view. She was home on a holiday from the USA; her excessive avoirdupois must have been a sore burden, but in the eyes of the young woman it was evidently a condition much to be desired, for she remarked: 'Isn't she lovely and fat?' This was a revelation to my wife, who asked: 'Would you like to be fat?' The reply, 'Oh, God, yes,' was startling in its emphasis and sincerity. Further conversation elicited the fact that her family was very worried because her mother did not put on flesh as she grew older. It was rather a disgrace to the family, and to hide the fact from neighbours they made her wear an abundance of heavy clothes which gave her figure the necessary bulk. The Blasket women evidently – attach as much importance to 'waxing fat' as did the Hebrews of old.

One old woman had a share in an Irish Hospital Sweepstake ticket and seemed surprised when I told her that I had never bought one; she thought I was either a simpleton or a very rich man. Fortunately I am neither. Like all gamblers, she had great plans in view if she won. She would: (1) get a set of false teeth; (2) paint her face to make herself look young; (3) buy a farm on the mainland; (4) buy a motor-car.

An old man, Blasket Island.

An old woman, Blasket Island.

During the summer months students stay on the island in order to learn the Irish language. Many of the islanders have no English and the dialect is Munster Irish, which is different from that spoken in Aran – which again is different to that spoken in Donegal, the latter being more akin to the Scotch Gaelic. These differences make it difficult to standardise the language; they are a serious drawback to its universal adoption and also create difficulties for those students who have to pass examinations to obtain positions in the Government services or to qualify for some of the professions.

One of my sons has stayed for lengthy periods on the island in order to obtain the conversational knowledge of Irish which is necessary for his profession of the Law. He took lessons from an old woman commonly known as 'old Peg.' One of her sons was killed while gathering 'scraw' turf on the side of the cliff; it came away suddenly and he was precipitated backwards over the edge. She is a remarkable woman who cannot write but has a wonderful gift of telling stories which range from prehistoric folk-tales down to the days of Daniel O'Connell, who lived in the nineteenth century. One scholar told me that he had collected over a hundred folk-tales on the island, some of which he had been able to trace through medieval times to their sources in the Orient. He told me that he thought they must have reached the Blaskets by the medium of travellers in the Middle Ages, but although I am not qualified to pass judgment on this question I cannot help thinking that their arrival on these islands dates back much further and that some of them have survived from the peoples who settled in Ireland in prehistoric times.

One old woman said she was afraid of purgatory and of *the two big dogs on the way*. Here we have a mixture of Catholic doctrine and a very early belief. Old Peg included in her repertoire variations of Aesop's fables, and the following story is a strange mixture of legend and the Land War of fifty years ago. I write it as it was taken down verbatim in Irish by my son.

DONAL NA NEELOUGH

It happened long ago that a young boy [all unmarried men in Ireland are called boys, irrespective of their age] was living in the parish of Il na Tearig. He was the son of a widow. He could not get any peace, there was always something going against him. He had a nice piece of ground, but if he had, he was annoyed by the patch of land, as he often had not the money to pay the rent.

His mother used to be down on him when he would not have brought sense and attention for his house and his portion of land. But he was a jolly and courageous boy and at whatever place there would be music and dancing there he would have to be.

One night he was coming home from Dingle and he had to travel by a lonely mountain pass that was called Maam Bhaile na Nah. It was said that a spirit used to be seen there, but the widow's son did not mind a spirit there or elsewhere. He was putting the road from him, for he was riding a fine horse. He saw an old woman walking on the road in front of him. The night was very late and he wondered what was the reason of an old woman being on the road at that time. When he came up to her he asked her what did she want so late as that. "Wisha pet," said she, "I have not too good a walk, and I am wearied by the road. If it please you to put me behind you on the back of the horse you will only have to bring me to the cross-roads."

"All right," said the widow's son, "get up on the bank." When she was on it he pulled the horse up to the bank; she sprang on to the back of the horse, then he spurred on the horse; but if he did, the horse could not go but slowly. There was the wonder of the world on him. What was the reason that the horse was not walking better? He struck it but that was all it could do.

It was only after a while that he perceived another horse travelling swiftly after him. The horse was coming up with him and he himself could only get the one slow progress out of his horse. As soon as the old woman perceived the other horse coming up with her she took one jump; she left the horse and faced down through the fields.

As soon as she was gone from the horse, courage and progress came in it.

"My curse on you, for an old woman," said the widow's son. "I suppose you are not any good. My horse was dead with you; there was not the champion of the hooves in you and look now that it is in them. There is the music and the life now."

At the time he was talking the other horse came up with him. There was a rider on its back and the widow's son never saw that man before. He spoke to the rider: "I thought," he said, "there was not anyone so late on the road as myself." "It is good luck for you that there is," said the rider. "Where is the woman you had on the horse?"

Wisha, I don't know where she is; when she observed you after her she jumped from the horse and went down towards a hollow from me."

"And do you know who she herself is?" asked the rider.

"I haven't the slightest knowledge," said the other man.

"My woe for ever you," said the rider. "That was a spirit, and you would be alive but as far as the cross-roads."

"You are a good man," said the son of the widow.

"She was afraid of me, anyway, and now, since the night is spent as it is, would you come with me? I need your help."

"I would not hesitate," said the widow's son, "but my mother will be anxious about me."

"She won't be," said the rider, "and I promise you that I will leave you here again without fail."

"All right," said the widow's son.

They turned on the road. The two horses were making sparks on the road. The widow's son did not know where he was going and he did not put any question to the other man. He did not speak a word until they reached Lough Leanee [one of the Killarney Lakes about fifty miles distant].

"Follow me," said the rider.

That is when the widow's son spoke. "How will I follow you?" he asked.

"Put your horse to the water's edge," said the other man. ' "It is a pity you did not kill me near my own house, without bringing me as far as this from home to die."

"Do not ask questions," said the rider. "There is no danger for you. Follow me."

Then the widow's son drove his horse and as soon as he came to the edge of the water there was a fine, broad, smooth road and it was not long till he reached the other side of the lough. They dismounted from the horses and went into a fine comfortable house where there was plenty of light, and everything that the widow's son looked upon was glistening in the light. There was a table in the kitchen and every sort of food set out on it. They sat down and ate and drank their fill. Then the rider told the widow's son to go down into the room and get some sleep. The widow's son took off his boots and went down to the room. There was a fine prepared bed there before him. He took off his clothes and stretched himself on it, but it was not long till he saw an annoying light in the corner of the room.

"Upon my soul," said he, "I'll be scalded; whatever is the fire in the room?"

He jumped out of his bed and went where the light was. He noticed that a sword stuck in a sheath was making the light. He tried to draw it out but the light was suddenly quenched.

He went to the bed again, but if he went the light was shining; he made another attempt to draw out the sword indeed, but the light went out.

"Indeed," he said in his own mind, "there is something upside down making this unfortunate light." ["Upside down" is a common expression used in Ireland to denote the abnormal.] There was no sleep falling on him as it should. He thought that the whole room was on fire. He jumped out of bed the third time and he seized the sword in his hand and he pulled it out all but a quarter of an inch. With that the light went out and from that on he did not see it. It was not long till the rider called him to get up quickly as they would be going back.

He rose and he put his clothes on him. The rider was ready before him. "Come," he said, "so that I may put you home."

They dragged out the two horses and they jumped on their backs and they held their faces towards the fine broad road that was going through the lough. Both sides of the road were full of fruit and of flowers of every colour.

The rider put a question to the widow's son: "Have you land?" he said.

"Yes," said the other man, "and I am tormented with it. The landlord is down on me demanding rents, and I haven't the rent to give him."

"Get down from the horse," said the rider, "and gather as many as you can of those green blooms on the bush beside you."

The widow's son got down and he filled a handkerchief with the blooms.

"When you will go home," said the rider, "preserve those, and don't have the bad luck to give one of them to any living person but only to the landlord – they will be money during twenty-four hours and then there will be nothing there but leaves."

And that is the time the widow's son put a question to him: "Who are you, good man?" he said.

"I am Donal O'Donoghue who is under a spell in this lough. That is my house you were in and it is a pity you did not succeed in doing the trick. If you had been so good that you had drawn the sword clean out of the sheath I would be putting you home, but perhaps I did not do the best thing when I took you with me-so that you would do that-when I saw you so brave about the old woman. She was a spirit," he said, "and you would have been dead at her on the cross-roads, but when she felt me after her she went with herself. And this is the name I am called by, Donal na Neelough, since I have that amount of power that I can put the evil spirits to flight."

By that time they were very close to the place where they met. They said their farewells and each went on his own way.

When the widow's son came home his mother was frightened as she had thought it was probable that the horse had killed him. He kept the handkerchief and all there was in it, but when the day of the rent came he took with him a fistful of the green leaves. As soon as he went to the office his fist was full of bank-notes. His rent was paid then, but when the money was counted later there was a deficit of the amount of the rent and nothing in its place but green leaves.

The landlord wondered who played the trick on him, but he found out in some way that it was the widow's son who had the false money. He brought him to law and on the day of the court the poor man was vexed ["vexed" is used in Ireland in the same sense as "worried"] without anything to save him.

But on the morning of the day of the court who came towards him but Dona! na Neelough. When the widow's son saw him he became angry. "My thousand curses on you," he said. "Isn't it you that put me in the fix? It is a pity for you that you didn't make a clean sweep of me that night we were in Lough Leane."

"Stop," said Donal. "I will repair the matter; give me ink and a piece of paper and I tell you there will not be danger for you."

The widow's son gave him the paper and the ink; he got down. beside the dyke and he drew a five-pound note on the paper-when he had done that he handed it to the widow's son.

"Here," said he, "there is not a judge or a lawyer that will find fault with that money." Then he left him and the widow's son went to the court-house.

When his case was called the judge asked him if he had any of the money about him. He said that there was and enough of it and he handed the five-pound note to the judge.

"That is the money I have, your honour," he said. "And if there is any fault in it I cannot help it." The people of the court examined it but they could not find any fault in it. The widow's son was let free and he afflicted the landlord with the green leaves. "He married a young Irish girl and he had a fine life from that on.

Many years ago when I was staying on the adjoining mainland a visitor (Miss Nicholls) lost her life in a gallant attempt to save from drowning an island woman who got into difficulties when bathing. I was told that shortly before the tragedy a 'phantom ship' had appeared, a sure forerunner of misfortune. The funeral procession of currachs across the Sound – there is no burial-place on the island – reminded me of a funeral that I saw in Venice where black gondolas take the place of the mourning coaches.

The islanders attend mass at Dunquin when weather permits, but there is not a sufficient number of currachs to carry everybody and most of the women and children remain behind. The parish priest visits the island once a year and it is a great honour to the house in which the temporary altar is erected. During the summer mass is frequently held by a visitor priest.

The island author, Thomás O' Crohan, Blasket Island.

The most celebrated person on the island is Tomás O'Crohan, an old man over seventy years of age who has written an autobiography in Irish. This work has been translated into English by Dr. Robin Flower and has had a great success both in the Irish and English versions. The English edition is entitled *The Islandman*. As a literary work it is outstanding, but not merely is it a marvellous literary achievement for an old peasant to accomplish, but it gives to the reader an intimate account which has never been surpassed of the life of a primitive community. Old Tomas is justifiably proud of his book and in the illustration he is seen holding a copy of it in his hands.

Some of the passages in his original manuscript were deleted in the edition issued for the use of schools by the Irish Government. One of the offending passages tells how, when gathering turf, he happened to be the only boy present and was 'set upon' by a number of girls engaged in the same occupation. They pulled his hair, scattered his turf, stampeded his donkey and generally gave him a rough time. He winds up the narrative of his adventure with the remark: 'This was the first time I was stung by the bees.'

The susceptibilities of our educational authorities are extraordinary. It is hard to credit that photographs of monkeys which on request I had submitted to a publisher for illustrations in a school reader were refused on the ground that they would probably give offence because they portrayed too great a likeness to humanity, and sketches were used which could not lend any support to the theory of evolution!

A poetical strain runs through the ordinary English spoken by the islanders. It is probably due to the translation from the Irish idiom of a people who are close to nature. We were one day discussing the weather with an old man. Gazing towards the west one could see the clouds over the Atlantic from which showers were falling here and there on the surface of the sea. 'The weather will not be good,' said he. 'I see the little feet of the showers.' Contrast this with 'a depression is approaching from the Atlantic; conditions will be unsettled.'

Another day when it was raining steadily I asked a woman if the weather would clear. She pointed to the south-west and remarked: 'There must be someone who is always crying over there,' a poetical way of expressing the fact that whilst the wind stayed in the south-west we need not expect the rain to cease.

Shortly before our visit there had been a discussion in the newspapers about a tax on bachelors, many people thinking that a special contribution to the revenue should be levied on unmarried men. The discussion certainly loaded the scales in favour of the ladies, for several engagements had already taken place. Any Irishman would rather risk matrimony than pay an extra tax even to his own native government. Coming from the centre of affairs at Dublin I was frequently asked about this tax, but I am afraid that I had to disappoint the inquirers, for I knew no more about the matter than the islanders themselves, and my reply, that I did not mind the tax as I was a married man with a family, gave the bachelors no comfort.

When a zealous police officer from the mainland some years ago tried to collect the dog tax on the island – every house has at least one dog, and the tax, then seven shillings and sixpence for each dog, would have been a great hardship – the old dogs past their work were thrown over the cliffs and the remainder were hidden at the far end of the island. Since then the attempt to collect the tax has not been repeated. The dogs are a necessity as sheep farming is the principal industry and, with lobster fishing and the revenue from visitors, is practically the only means of obtaining the cash necessary to pay for the necessities of life which they have to purchase.

Frequent losses are incurred by sheep falling over the cliffs; they clamber down the face of the cliffs, which are steep, and often they cannot get up again, and are either starved, or more frequently they are killed in frantic endeavours to retrace their steps. On one occasion when a sheep belonging to the tailor of the island was cut severely by a fall, he put three stitches in its jaw with his ordinary needle and thread and the wound healed.

As well as the ubiquitous donkey, there are a few horses on the island – horses which lead a peaceful, easy-going existence far from all traffic problems and noise of civilisation. The islanders still speak of the disturbance caused by Lindbergh's aeroplane when he passed over the island during his famous crossing of the Atlantic. The boys thought it was an eagle and the horses stampeded and were so frightened that it took several days to round them up.

During the lobster season a boat comes from France every fortnight. When she is seen in the distance messengers are sent to men working in their plots. There is then great activity in the launching of currachs, and by the time she has arrived the lobsters have been collected from the floating tanks and the currachs are waiting for her. When we were there one family were paid £7 10s. for their share.

When the boat first began to call there was a difficulty in carrying out the business transactions. As the captain of the vessel spoke French and the islanders Irish neither party understood the other, and neither of them was able to talk fluently in English, which was the sole connecting link. These difficulties were eventually solved and the island men appreciate the value of the market at their very doors, as before the French boat called they had to sail about fifteen miles to Dingle in order to sell their lobsters for transportation to London. I was told that the French sailors were 'decent men,' an Irish expression that denotes the height of respectability. At one time they sold waterproofs very cheaply but the revenue authorities got word of this and they were fined a hundred pounds for selling goods on which import duty had not been paid.

The population of the island is about two hundred, between thirty and forty of whom are schoolchildren attending the national school in charge of a mistress. The school is sometimes closed, as it is always difficult to obtain a teacher, who must speak Irish fluently and be content to live in this backwater, out of touch with the world and deprived of any company of her own social standing. It seems strange that there are no rats although many vessels have been wrecked in the vicinity and the island shares with Inishmurray this distinction as well as the fact that it has no church, clergy, shop or public-house.

There is little flat ground; one always seems to be walking uphill, and this rising ground culminates in Croagh Martin, a hill nine hundred feet high, separated from another eminence, Slieve Donagh, by an open valley. It is a wonderful experience to walk along the top of the high ridge which is the backbone of the island, and from which the ground slopes rapidly to the great jagged cliffs forming the boundaries on the north and south sides. The island is really a mountain ridge which in some parts is not more than a quarter of a mile wide.

The hill named Slieve Donagh on the maps should really be called Slieve Dun, because it takes its name from a fort or dun on the summit. I could find no reference to this dun in any of the archaeological journals, so I think it wise to put the details on record even though they may be dull matter for many of my readers. The dun is situated on a rocky eminence; on the north side is a small cliff, below which is a grassy slope strewn with boulders, descending at a steep angle to the sheer cliffs. On this side the nature of the terrain forms an efficient protection and on the south or landward side, where the slope of the ground is less acute, a fosse or vallum has been excavated, the inner bank of which is composed of a steep, high bank or loose wall of stones which is now partially overgrown with turf.

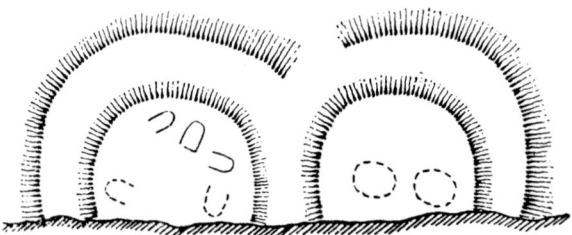

Diagramatic plan of dun (fort) on Sleive Donagh.

The fort consists of two separate enclosures, a rather unique feature, with a vallum between them. These two enclosures have only one entrance through the outer fosse that surrounds both of them. The general plan can be understood from the rough sketch illustrated, and would lead one to the conclusion that originally there was only one enclosure and that the dun was subsequently enlarged by the extension of the outer vallum and the addition of a second enclosure. Inside the western enclosure are the remains of two large circular cloghauns, and in the eastern enclosure are the remains of five oval or rectangular cells.

In addition to the ruined cloghauns in this fort there are ruined cloghauns of an early construction on the flatter ground near the western end of the island, and in the village there is a modern beehive cell which is used for storage purposes.

There is not much tillage on the island, only sufficient crops for their own needs being grown by the islanders, as there is no external market possible; but they possess about eight hundred sheep and a fair number of cattle.

On the occasion of our visit we had the good luck to see a large cow shipped to the mainland in one of the currachs. It is a hazardous job which is only undertaken when the sea is very calm, and the currach containing the cow is always accompanied by another boat, for should the beast struggle on the journey the currach containing it would probably be capsized.

Before I saw the performance I wondered how the beast could be transferred to the boat without causing damage, since the ribs and bottom of the framework consisting of thin laths with no protection between them except the tarred canvas through which a hoof could easily

Shipping Livestock: cow on harbour slip, Blasket Island.

Shipping livestock: cow in a currach, Blasket Island.

penetrate. On occasions of this sort the owner of the beast is helped by his friends and this sharing of tasks is a very pleasant feature of island life.

The procedure is simple when one knows how to carry it out, but requires considerable strength and skill. Large bundles of bracken are placed in the bottom of the canoe and a rope is tied around the head of the animal, which is then thrown off its feet and falls on a pile of bracken on the slip. Its legs are then tied and it is pulled and shoved over the edge of the slip into the boat in such a position that its feet are least likely to do damage to men or boat and the animal itself is fairly comfortable. If in a strained position it might struggle with disastrous results.

Two men use the oars and a third man in the stern of the boat gives his whole attention to the beast. The rate of progress is slow, for the load is very heavy and great care must be taken in the handling of the currach.

Talking one day with the oldest man on the island I was asked if I had ever been on any other islands. When I informed him that I had stayed several times on the Aran Islands, 'Ah!' said he, 'Aran is a fine island, there is no blast on the potatoes, and I hear there are three public-houses and two chapels there.' So does our environment colour our outlook on life. To this simple Blasket man, dwelling in a spot without shop, church or public-house, the fact that another island, although bleak and rocky, possessed these amenities made it a desirable place in which to live.

At the risk of repetition I would again emphasise the natural courtesy and friendliness which I have always received from the simple folk who live on our islands. This friendliness is well expressed in a letter from a Blasket friend to whom I sent photographs which I had taken when staying there.

> DEAR MR. MASON,
> Many thanks for the nice photographs you send me. I got them about three or four weeks ago and I was awfully glad to get them. I should have written to you long ago, only I was very busy. I gave each person his own photograph and they were all glad to get them. I gave the schoolmistress her own ones and she was very pleased with them. There was a whole lot of visitors here this summer and we had singing and dancing almost every night. The Island was crowded. "Oh," we had a great time with them.
>
> How is Mrs. Mason and all the family? Hoping they are all well, as we are at present, thank God.
>
> I am going to send some of my own photographs to my sisters in America. My father and mother send you all their best wishes. Good-bye. With kind thoughts from...

In the church where I worship I heard, in October 1933, a sermon which made a great impression on me. I forget the text, which is of no importance, but I do remember the preacher stating that 'the greatest gentility is often found in the humblest homes,' and he proceeded to point out that our Lord was probably reared in a house with but a single room. This fact is brought out in some of His parables; for instance, in Matthew v. 15: 'Neither do men light a candle and put it under a bushel, but on a candlestick, and it giveth light unto all that are in the house.' If the house envisaged by our Lord had more than one room how could the candle give light to all within the dwelling? Again in Luke xi. 7: 'The door is now shut and my children are with me in bed.' Our Lord speaks of a humble home with one large bed.

Let no thought of superiority or snobbishness enter one's mind when thinking about these island people, for if it does one should examine oneself for the beam that is in one's own eye.

Chapter Fifteen
The Skelligs

In the previous chapters I have written about islands in which a hardy fisher-folk eke out a living, but the Skelligs are inhabited only by lighthouse men and wild birds.

The Skelligs, which lie off the coast of Kerry about ten miles from the mainland, consist of two rocky islets, Skellig Michael and Little Skellig. By courtesy of the Commissioners of Irish Lights, myself and two of my sons were permitted to stay in the dwellings of the light-keepers, situated on the larger island.

About 9.00 am we embarked on the relief vessel which set out from Knightstown Harbour on the island of Valentia carrying supplies to the lighthouses on this part of the coast. Proceeding in a north-westerly direction we arrived at the Tearaght, a precipitous rock some hundreds of feet high. The supplies were hoisted to a platform cut out of the solid rock by tackle lowered to the deck of the vessel, which, on account of the Atlantic swell, could not approach too closely to the landing-place.

A small boat was lowered from the ship, and by jumping when it rode on the top of a wave we were able to land. This was rather exciting as, although the waves did not break, the rise and fall were considerable. The sailors watched the waves and, when they gave the word to jump immediate action was necessary, as a delay of a couple of seconds meant all the difference between safety and disaster. One of our party hesitated and would have fallen into the sea, with a great risk of being crushed between the boat and the concrete wall, but for the prompt action of one of the men, who seized him around the thighs and pulled him back into the boat. I confess that, although he was a good swimmer, I had for a moment a spasm of fear as I saw him suspended, his feet on the gunwale of the boat and his fingers on the wall of the landing-stage. The boat was falling rapidly as the wave receded and in another second he would have been precipitated into the sea.

The Great Skellig Rock, Skellig Michael. The X marks the position of the monastery.

We all managed to land and I was glad to be on terra firma for the half-hour during which supplies were being landed from the vessel. I am a fairly good sailor, but I was feeling somewhat squeamish and hoped that the break in the journey would put me right. This optimism was in vain, for shortly after leaving the Tearaght I became violently ill. I have crossed the Irish Sea and the English Channel in gales, but I have never been so prostrated with *mal de mer* as on this journey. I felt like those unfortunate people depicted in our humorous journals who are so miserable that they do not care what may happen to the vessel.

Ever since this experience I fail to see why such miseries of mankind should be the butt of humorists – to them I would apply the prescription of Gilbert and Sullivan and make the punishment fit the crime.

The vessel rolled so much that I thought her bottom must be round in shape. The captain, Florence O'Driscoll, took pity on me and put his cabin at my disposal, where he brought me a cup of tea made with sweet condensed milk. This, combined with the smell of the machine-oil used in the engines, was the last straw and I spent the remainder of the journey lying flat on the deck.

When we were approaching the Blaskets the skipper asked me if I would like him to sail between them so that I would get a good view. The depth of my misery may be gauged by my reply: 'For God's sake get to the Skelligs by the shortest route.'

We arrived at Skellig Michael about three o'clock in the afternoon, having traversed thirty miles of the open Atlantic. I was very weak when I landed and only at six o'clock did I venture on a cup of tea and a dry biscuit, my only food since eight in the morning.

There are three landing-places on Skellig Michael so that if, owing to the state of the sea, it is not possible to utilise the principal slip, a landing may be effected at one of the other places which face in different directions. If the light-keepers are not able to land in a small boat they are hoisted up by a noosed cable lowered by a long crane from the cliff. On many occasions the Commissioners of Irish Lights have landed in this fashion when on a tour of inspection. We were fortunate in being able to land with comparative ease on the slip, whence we proceeded along the ascending path, a quarter of a mile in length, cut by the lighthouse engineers along the face of the cliff to the keepers' quarters.

Skellig Michael was dedicated to St. Michael, the patron saint of high places. It consists of two high peaks, with a sheer drop of more than six hundred feet to the Atlantic. Between them is a hollow space known as Christ's Saddle; this is the only comparatively flat ground on the island, situated at a height of four hundred feet. Wherever one wanders on this sea-girt rock one is faced with stupendous cliffs. The island is a drowned mountain of which only the peaks remained above water when the lowering of the land surface took place in past geological epochs.

From early historical times, probably the sixth century, it was the seat of a monastery. The following words were written by the late T. J. Westropp in 1905. They were probably true of the medieval period and I can vouch for their truth in this twentieth century: 'It seems so very lonely, so very far from even that quiet world, whose blue, grey and purple headlands bound the eastern view, that it takes little stretch of imagination to see what a city of refuge such a place must have been to ardent, self-conscious men fleeing from the temptations of great cities and decaying civilisation of the old world and even from the missionary labours of men of the type of Columbanus, to fight with such sin as they brought with them, unstrengthened by the evil outside them.'

I went to the island in order to study and photograph the remains of this early Christian settlement, and stayed on it for nearly a week. I spent a portion of my time

The road to tthe lighthouse, Skellig Michael.

seated on the summit of one of the peaks overlooking the little monastery. The weather was perfect. and, gazing over the sea, I spent many hours in contemplation of the wonderful beauty of the panorama which lay before me. The white bodies of the gannets gleamed brightly in the sun as they performed their aerial evolutions. Pausing anon in their flight to descend through the air with the rapidity of a falling stone, they struck the water and disappeared below the surface of the sea in their search for food.

Occasionally a fulmar petrel appeared to grace the scene.

He is different from all the other sea birds, the difference being not merely in the shape of his wings or his colour, but also in his flight. Until I had seen the fulmar in flight I had thought the kittiwake gull to be the most beautiful of all our birds when in the air, but the flight of the fulmar surpasses even that of the kittiwake. It is the embodiment of aerial grace. In writing of the evolutions of the fulmar one hesitates to use the word 'flight.' The word seems to denote a physical effort which is out of place in a description of the perfect union which seems to exist between this bird and the atmosphere. It is true that one notices occasionally two or three beats of the wing; this serves but as a reminder that one is observing a living creature and not an aerial being that floats through the air. The flight of the fulmar cannot be described, it must be seen, for in no other way can one get any idea of its beauty as the bird rises or descends in graceful curves without apparent effort.

Two miles distant one could see the Little Skellig glistening white in the sunshine by reason of its countless sea birds. Here and there one saw the brown sails of a fishing boat standing out in strong contrast to the deep blue of the sea and in the distance the glorious panorama of the Kerry Mountains, rich in colours that varied as the shadows of passing clouds fell on them.

The occasional cry of a bird and the murmur of the sea six hundred feet below were the only sounds to penetrate the peace of this place. The sea did not disturb; it had a soothing effect and I felt that the monks certainly had a perfect retreat in which they could devote themselves to a life of meditation. Even the winter gales which howl around the rocky pinnacles of the island, although fearsome, must induce a feeling of reverence in

The monastery and monks' garden, Skellig Michael.

man and make him realise his own insignificance in the face of the tremendous forces of nature.

It was midsummer when we were on the island, but I got from a light-keeper some idea of the terrific gales and seas which occur in the winter. He told me that frequently the waves break over the lighthouse, which is nearly two hundred feet above the sea, and such is the force of the wind that the large parapet stones, measuring about three feet by two feet by four inches, are sometimes blown from the top of the wall which protects the edge of the road to the lighthouse.

The fog-signal station is some distance from the lighthouse, in a very exposed position four hundred feet high, so an electrical apparatus which could be worked from the lighthouse was designed in order to save the operator from exposure. It was a great boon and worked well for some time until a short circuit occurred and three hundred maroons [signal rockets] were exploded simultaneously. Having heard at close quarters the sound caused by the explosion of one signal I cannot even imagine the noise caused by the explosion of three hundred. It must have been terrific. In the words of one of the men, 'It nearly lifted the island out of the sea.'

Since this mishap the electrical contrivance has been discarded.

The light-keepers have a couple of goats which are generally located in some almost inaccessible position at milking time. With bated breath I have watched the men retrieve these perverse animals and came to the conclusion that the men were as sure-footed as the goats themselves. Since watching the goats on the Skelligs I have learned the real depth and significance attached to the expression 'a giddy goat' that one hears applied to a foolish person. There is no place in the scheme of nature for a giddy goat.

St. Michael's Pillar showing position of the last station..

Throughout the centuries the island was a place of pilgrimage. To reach the last station the pilgrim had to squeeze through a narrow cleft in the rock called the Needle's Eye from which a short steep ascent led to a rock projecting over the cliff. This rock, ten feet long, is only two feet wide, and the pilgrim, sitting astride it, manages to project himself forward until he can kiss a cross which is inscribed on the stone. This is surely a test of penitence and faith, for the pilgrim is suspended in the air with the sea seven hundred feet below.

On the occasion of my visit I was still suffering from the effects of synovitis in my knee and could not attempt the perilous feat.

The Gregorian system for calculating the date of Easter was adopted by most of the countries of continental Europe in 1582, but it was not adopted officially in

Ireland until 1782, with the result that in some 'out of the world' districts Easter was celebrated according to the old method of reckoning.

A modern analogy can be found in 'summer time' which was adopted during the war in England, but except for legal business or railway time-tables it is ignored in most parts of rural Ireland, and in the case of country funerals the words 'old time' or 'new time' are always inserted after the announcement in the local newspapers.

Summer time is a blessing to townsmen or industrial workers, but is unsuitable to an agricultural community and the rural Irishman has no use for it. He scathingly calls it 'Lloyd George's time,' and speaks of the old system as 'God Almighty's time.'

I am not sure if this change in the calendar in the eighteenth century is responsible for an old

The Needle's Eye, Skellig Michael.

custom; its origin may date as far back as the seventh or eighth centuries, when the theologians of the Early Celtic Church disputed the method of fixing the date of Easter, but the fact remains that the period of Lent commenced later on the Skelligs than on the mainland, with the consequence that in former times parties who were too late to get married on the mainland could still enter the bonds of holy matrimony on the Skelligs. This was the origin of the rhyming satirical leaflets called 'Skellig Lists,' 'the poetasters endeavouring in the most absurd manner to join the most incongruous pairs together.' These lists were sold on the mainland on Shrove Tuesday, but as their contents often gave offence the influence of the Church has caused their gradual disappearance, to the great relief of the elderly spinsters of County Kerry.

The island is about half a mile long and in some parts nearly a quarter of a mile wide. As one approaches it one can see through a pair of field-glasses the beehive cells of the ancient monastery, 'clinging like swallows' nests' to a ridge of rock more than five hundred feet in height, and near the summit of the northern peak – 'the most western of Christ's fortresses in the ancient world' – one can only marvel at the inward force which urged men to attempt the building of a religious establishment in such a place. The actual position on the island was well chosen, for the beehive cells built without mortar in the sixth and seventh centuries are still intact – a remarkable tribute to the foresight and skill of the builders. A later church built with mortar is in a ruinous condition, but the simple cells and oratories have withstood the Atlantic gales for more than a thousand years. One would imagine that a settlement like this would offer no inducement to marauders but

In the monastery, Skellig Michael.

The monks' cemetery, Skellig Michael.

such was not the case, for we read that the Vikings in 823, disappointed in their search for loot, carried off in revenge one of the monks.

The simple life of the community, devoid of earthly ambitions, must have impressed even these fierce pirates, for we read that later a Norse king, Olaf, was baptized here.

The modern roadway cuts across the old way to the monastery and reduces the labour of the ascent, but even now it is a stiff climb up the six hundred rough steps which lead to the enclosure. We reach first the small plateau called Christ's Saddle whence the pathway of steps winds its way through fantastic pinnacles of rock, and in due course we arrive at the wall of the cashel. This wall is built up in many parts from a lower rock ledge and acts as a retaining wall for the scanty soil which served as a garden for the monastery.

When I first arrived at the monastery I sat down to rest and think, thrilled and excited by the thought that I had at last reached a spot visited by few, a place which I had often wished to see and photograph, hallowed and sanctified by centuries of piety; a spot where one could see the most perfect example in Christendom of an early, simple, religious establishment, where, far from telephones, motor-cars and business worries a man born in the nineteenth century is able to visualise the life of an early Christian community and to feel like them a complete detachment from the distractions of ordinary life.

To an ordinary man this type of life is not possible, nor do I think it desirable. A righteous man doing good work and setting an example in his life amongst his business or professional or social acquaintances and friends has a far greater influence for good than if he retires permanently to some isolated retreat where his meditation and exercises, whilst benefiting himself spiritually, seem to be somewhat selfish; he cannot have the influence for good in the world which a more intimate contact with his fellow men would produce. But, whilst this is my conscientious belief, I also certainly believe that an occasional withdrawal from the rush of modern life to an isolated place where one can think and meditate cannot fail to be of great benefit, mental, spiritual and physical, to all men. It helps one to regain a more balanced outlook on life and to realise that the irritating details about which we fret and worry are insignificant items in the eternal scheme.

The remains consist of six beehive cells, two oratories, two wells, a number of rude crosses and inscribed slabs and the later Church of St. Michael.

The majority of the cells are round externally but the interiors are rectangular, the method of construction being similar to that described in earlier chapters dealing with Inishmurray or Aran; the workmanship, however, is much

Interior of rectangular cell, Skellig Michael.

better. The illustrations give a good idea of this remarkable settlement – a much better idea indeed than is possible by a verbal description. The illustration of an interior was photographed in the only rectangular cell and shows how well these early builders fitted the stones together at the corners. One can also see how the interspaces between the large stones were filled by the insertion of small flat stones.

Whilst waiting inside one of these cells until our eyes became accustomed to the dim light we heard peculiar noises, which on investigation we found to be caused by stormy petrels, 'Mother Carey's chickens,' which were nesting in holes in the walls. We had never previously seen these birds at such close quarters and could not help wondering how such a small bird managed to exist on the ocean, for it only comes to land for nesting purposes.

The two small oratories are rectangular in form, with a simple window on the eastern side. One of these oratories is outside the main enclosure and local tradition calls it 'the prison'; possibly it was reserved for the use of those guilty of very grievous sin. In the other oratory, which is situated inside the cashel wall, there is a small stone altar on which one can see modern offerings left by pilgrims. I noticed several coins in addition to rosary beads, and other articles of a religious nature.

The most pathetic place in the settlement is the small cemetery of the monks. It is situated immediately behind the oratory and is formed of soil about four feet deep, which had evidently been collected and placed in this spot, for nowhere on the island is there soil of sufficient depth to permit of hygienic burial. The earth is kept in place by a retaining wall of loose stones and many rude crosses and slabs with incised crosses mark the resting-places of these early Christians.

We were surprised to find an ancient well in the monastery. It was the existence of this supply of water that made the settlement possible, but one certainly would not expect to find it on a rocky island nearly six hundred feet above the sea:

The water for the light-keepers is collected from the roofs of the buildings whence it runs into large covered tanks. The roofs are covered with the droppings of the sea birds, so the water is not run into the tanks until the rain has been falling for some hours, and has consequently washed them clean.

During the nesting season there are multitudes of birds, including some of the rarer species, nesting on the island; in addition to the common sea fowl, such as puffins, guillemots, gulls, etc., we saw the peregrine falcon and the chough, and of course the fulmar and stormy petrels which I have previously mentioned.

The fulmar nests on a narrow ledge on the face of the cliff six hundred feet high, the nest, if one can call it a nest, consisting of small flat stones on which the bird lays its solitary white egg. The embodiment of all grace when flying, it is the most ungainly of birds when on the land; its proper sphere is on the sea or in the air and it only comes to land during the breeding season. If one approaches it too closely it ejects an evil-smelling oily liquid which is very difficult to remove from one's clothes. The small stormy petrel also ejects an oily liquid. The oil is so offensive that it is an efficient weapon of defence, although I am not sure whether its ejection is a defensive action or merely due to a nervous reflex.

We wished to pay a visit to the Little Skellig where, through our field-glasses, we could see thousands of gannets nesting, so when a few days later the motor-boat which we had ordered arrived with several passengers who wished to pay a visit to the monastery I arranged with the men to bring us to the Little Skellig and to call for us on their way home.

The sea was not calm, but a friend who had come on the motor-boat had tied his very small punt to its stern and we were able, after much searching, to land from it on to a narrow ledge from which we hoped to be able to climb to the top of the rock. This hope was in vain, as we found the rocks impossible to climb, and for a couple of hours we were held prisoners in this restricted place. Then the wind changed, the tide turned and we became really anxious as we watched the rising sea, which now broke into the small cove where we had landed.

When the motor-boat eventually came in sight it could not approach the island and the journey had to be made in the small punt, which was only able to accommodate one passenger in addition to the oarsman. The journeys to and fro were not without danger and I breathed a sigh of relief when the last member of our party of three was safe on the large motor-boat. It was an anxious time. I was doubtful if we could get away from the rock, and the prospect of being marooned with the gannets did not appeal to me. I learned later that no relief to the Skelligs Lighthouse was possible for six weeks after this date, so we had even a closer escape than I realised at the time.

Our troubles were not yet over, however, for something went wrong with the engine and for nearly an hour the boat was tossing in a rough sea; eventually repairs were effected and we arrived at Valentia Harbour about 10.00 pm. All's well that ends well, but I shall not forget my trip to the Skelligs.

A gannet (solan goose) on nest, Saltee Island.

Chapter Sixteen

The Saltee Island, Co. Wexford

As a boy I 'devoured' the story of *Robinson Crusoe*; I read it several times and, like most healthy boys, thought that the summit of human happiness and experience was reached by that remarkable person. The story of *Robinson Crusoe* will never die; it appeals in an extraordinary manner to the instincts of all boys – except of course the namby-pambies or the goody-goodies who never do anything worthwhile in this world – and men, as our wives often remind us, are merely big boys. Imagine therefore my pleasure when a celebrated scientist invited me to join a small party that he was organising for a visit to the Great Saltee Island. That was nearly thirty years ago, and since then I have visited the island many times.

The island is five miles from land. It lies off the south coast of County Wexford, just around the extreme south-east corner of Ireland. When one looks at a map of bird migration one finds that it lies right on one of the great lines of migration when in spring and autumn our feathered friends change their habitat. It is not now inhabited but was once farmed. The farmer could not get labourers to stay on the island, which has now reverted to a primitive condition and is, I think, the most wonderful resort of birds in Great Britain or Ireland.

The local Civic Guards (police) keep a close watch on all visitors and ensure that the provisions of the Wild Birds Protection Act are not infringed.

The port of embarkation is the pretty seaside village of Kilmore Quay from which a boat can be hired. On the occasion of my first visit we were storm-stayed for four days. Our supply of bread and butter was nearly exhausted, but we had no fear of starvation as rabbits were plentiful and sea birds' eggs, if not exactly palatable, would at least allay the pangs of hunger. We also knew that a drinkable and nourishing soup could be made from the flesh of the smaller green cormorant – the shag – but this prospect, although seriously debated, was not received enthusiastically.

South side of Saltee Island (bird sanctuary), County Wexford.

There is no harbour on the island, and when the wind is blowing from a northerly direction landing is difficult and dangerous. The delay in our return, although a source of anxiety to our families, did not otherwise worry us with the exception of one of our party who was a college professor and had to be in Dublin to conduct examinations. By good fortune the wind changed during the night and we embarked at 6.30 am the next morning, so the situation was saved.

Before the war and our own Irish 'troubles' I paid many subsequent visits, and when at last one was again able, after a hiatus of nearly ten years, to live a normal life, I was considering ways and means of visiting the island, this time with my wife and four sons, when the problem was solved in an unexpected fashion.

Chatting with some friends over coffee one of the party who was in the motor business asked if one of us was a 'sportsman'? Cautiously I asked: 'What do you mean by a sportsman?' When I was a young man the word generally designated a person who actively practised some athletic exercise, but in recent years the meaning has been degraded, so that it embraces bookmakers' victims and gamblers of every description.

'Will you buy a car for thirty pounds?' 'What's wrong with it?'

'Nothing is wrong with it.'

'Was it looted?' (We were still living in the aftermath of the civil war.)

'No, it wasn't looted.'

'Well, if it will bring me up the hill to my cottage in the mountains I will buy it.'

It brought me up the hill, and so I became the possessor of a 1913 Ford car [Model T] with a large English-made body and a wonderful engine. I had no fault to find with my purchase. I ran it for four years and then sold it for three pounds to a country blacksmith who converted it into a lorry, and even in 1934 I saw it on the road carrying loads of gravel.

Within three weeks after my purchase we were en route to the Saltee Island, the car loaded with blankets and all sorts of equipment necessary for six persons who intended to live on a desert island for ten days and whose stay might, by stress of weather, be more prolonged.

We were able to procure groceries at Kilmore and did not carry these with us but we brought bottled milk, and this was a wise precaution, as when the bottles were immersed in a well the contents kept fresh for nearly a week. I made out a list of necessities and showed it to my wife who informed me that it seemed all right, except that I had omitted to include soap, an item easily overlooked by a mere man, but of prime importance to the mother of four boys.

Sacks of wood fibre for bedding were sent in advance by rail to the nearest station, which we had some difficulty in finding as all the signposts had been thrown down or reversed in order to mislead the 'Black and Tans' during the 'war,' and had not yet been re-erected. We were delayed in Kilmore Quay for three days before it was possible to attempt the landing. Before we were ready to sail two rabbit trappers who had been weatherbound for a week arrived from the island. One of them told me that when, three weeks previously, they had taken up residence in the old farm-house they were very much overrun by rats, which did not seem to fear humans. On my previous visits I had often seen and heard rats but they never interfered much with our comfort or with our food, which was kept in a closed box.

The trappers assured me that before they left matters had improved considerably, so I thought it wiser to say nothing to my wife about the rats although I was not easy in my conscience.

The trappers had killed 157 rats in three days. Their method was simple. An old door was laid on the ground and then propped up in an inclined position by a wooden pole, to which a rope was attached, this rope being carried to an upper window. Heavy stones were placed on top of the door, tempting bait being placed underneath it, and when a number of rats had collected for the banquet one of the men pulled the rope, with the result that the door with its heavy load of stones fell on the rats and squashed them flat.

I was glad the trappers had been on the island immediately previous to our visit, as we were not troubled, and when we had returned home I relieved my conscience. My want of candour was justified, for my wife said that if she had even thought of the possibility of rats nothing would have induced her to stay on the island, but as matters turned out we had a perfectly glorious holiday.

On our journey across we noticed enormous numbers of jelly-fish, varying in size from the size of a penny to about a foot in diameter. Their colouring was beautiful, some of the blue shades being particularly delicate. The boatmen assured us that such numbers of jelly-fish were a sure sign of a fine summer, and this forecast was true because the following months – it was now June – were the finest that we had experienced in Ireland for many years.

Whilst I went for a ramble with the boys my wife remained behind to unpack and prepare the evening meal. On our return she asked me where I had put the cutlery as she was unable to find it. Imagine the consternation when I confessed that I had put it in one of the pockets of the car after an al fresco lunch on our journey down and had forgotten all about it. No knives, forks or spoons for at least a week! We managed by using boy scout knives and pen-knives and metal tent-pegs for forks, and – necessity is the mother of invention – we fabricated useful spoons of various sizes by binding limpet shells into the split ends of pieces of wood which we got from the box sent by the grocer to hold our food. The boys really enjoyed using these weapons at their meals – it was more like *Robinson Crusoe* than civilised spoons and forks.

During the late spring and summer myriads of sea birds resort to the island for breeding purposes and these are the great attraction, but in addition to these many other birds can be seen. We made a list of those we observed on various occasions and give it here for record purposes:

*Magpie	Partridge	*Great Black Back
*Jackdaw	Waxwing	*Lesser Black Back
*Blackbird	*Peregrine Falcon	*Herring Gull
*Swallow	*Shelduck	*Kittiwake
*Wren	*Mallard	*Manx Shearwater
*Lark	Redshank	*Puffin
*Meadow Pipit	*Ringed Plover	Razorbill
Rock Pipit	Curlew	Guillemot
*Wheatear	Sandwich Tern	*Ringed Guillemot
Robin	Lapwing	Gannet
Rock Pigeon	*Oyster Catcher	*Cormorant
Chough	*Fulmar Petrel	*Shag
Hoodie Crow		

Total – 37 varieties.

I do not suggest that all of these birds actually nest on the island, but the vast majority do. From actual observation I know that thirty species (marked with asterisks) breed or have bred there and possibly we failed to observe others.

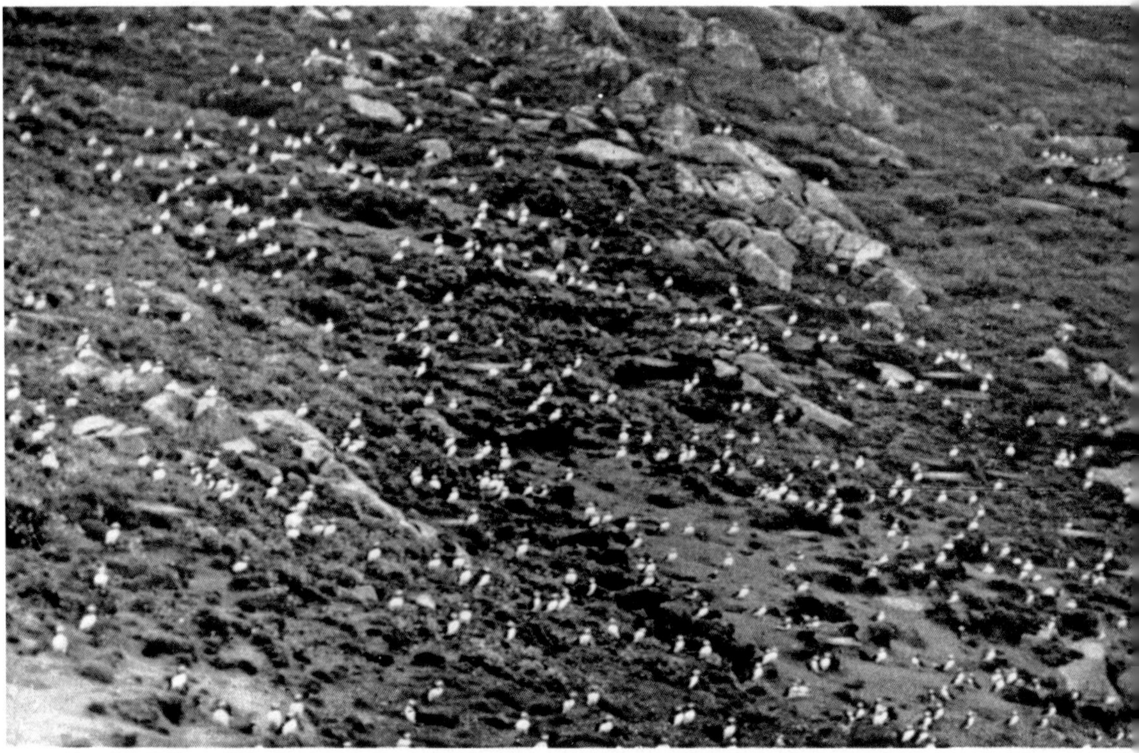

Puffins outside nesting-holes in foggy weather, Saltee Island.

Young peregrine falcons, Saltee Island.

The island is only about a mile and a half long and varies in width from a quarter to three-quarters of a mile, so one can realise that it is a wonderful place for studying bird life. I have known the island for nearly thirty years and can state that during that period the number of birds have increased considerably. The only species that seem to have decreased in numbers are the puffins.

During my last three visits I did not see the peregrine falcon which formerly rested on the cliffs. I have no doubt that systematic robbing of its eggs caused it to desert the island, but now the Wild Birds Protection Act is in force and the Civic Guards take such an interest in its application that I hope the peregrine will return.

On a fine day we made an approximate estimate of the numbers of birds floating on the surface of the sea and it came to 750,000 [see note to third edition page 12]. This was a conservative rough count which we made by counting the numbers in a section and multiplying it to give an estimate only of those birds which were on the sea on the south side of the island, and we took no account of the birds on land or on the sea surrounding the east, north and west sides.

Since then the birds have increased enormously. Portions of the cliffs and even the boulders projecting from the boulder clay which were formerly unfrequented are now so congested with bird life that there is a housing, or rather a site, shortage for nesting purposes. Taking all these facts into consideration I believe that a fair estimate should now place the numbers at about two and a half or three million birds. The number seems incredible but the estimate is seriously made after due consideration and many observations spread over a long period of years.

The Puffin

A puffin, Saltee Island

Of all the sea birds my favourite is the puffin, called by sailors the sea-parrot on account of its large, brightly coloured beak. The greater portion of this fantastic beak is shed when the breeding season is over, and the bird returns to the sea where it lives until it comes to land for nesting purposes in the following summer. It is an inoffensive, peaceable little bird but when aroused it fights savagely. I have seen two of them in mortal combat, each with its opponent's throat fiercely held in its beak, roll over the edge of a cliff, never relaxing their grip as they tumbled through the air into the sea, where they drowned each other.

They nest in holes and in many places they have driven the rabbits out of their burrows, which they utilise. In some parts of the island it is almost impossible to walk without sinking up to one's knees, the ground is so honeycombed with puffins' burrows. They lay a single white egg, remarkably large for such a small bird – indeed nearly as big as a cormorant's egg. If one inserts a flash-lamp inside a blown egg one can see spots which are not apparent when the egg is viewed in the ordinary way, and this leads one to surmise that possibly at some stage of its history the bird had laid its egg in the open where it was camouflaged by spots to hide it from observation.

The nesting-hole is always on ground sloping towards the sea, for the puffin cannot rise like a land bird and must 'taxi' like an aeroplane before it rises in the air. If it is startled when standing on the edge of a cliff it simply launches itself into the air, but if it is some distance from the edge it stumbles and falls in a ludicrous manner in its haste to get away.

It has no real tail – its stern is torpedo-shaped and it steers its way through the air by its little orange-coloured webbed feet.

The true habitat of these members of the auk family is the sea, and their agility under water is in striking contrast to their clumsiness on land. I have watched them in pursuit of fish under the water and marvelled at the performance. When feeding their mate on the nest or their young they come to land with a row of small fish or fry held firmly across their beak. I have counted six fish thus held; one would imagine that in opening their beaks to catch the later fish they would lose those already caught, but a provision of nature prevents this disaster-the edge of the beak has rough serrations which prevent the fish from slipping.

In foggy weather they assemble in multitudes on the edge of the cliffs and around their nesting-holes, but when the weather is fine they spend most of their day on the sea, returning to land in the evening, replete with fish, to enjoy the sunshine on the rocks.

There must be some telepathic communication between birds, otherwise how can one account for the simultaneous flight of numbers of puffins? Often when watching in the evening I have seen hundreds of these birds suddenly, without any previous warning, launch themselves into the air; they would then fly along the shore several times, wheeling with military precision and return to land with the same spontaneity as when they departed.

An American magazine published many years ago the following lines which aptly describe the puffin:

> There once was a provident puffin
> Who ate all the fish he could stuff in.
> Said he, "Tis my plan
> To eat when I can,
> When there's nuffin to eat I eat nuffin.'
> [Oliver Herford in *The Century Magazine*.
> Vol. LXXXIII, December 1911, No. 2, p. 319.]

The Guillemot

The guillemot is also a member of the auk family and is even more ungainly on land than the puffin – I should really say rocks instead of land, for it never goes farther than the sea cliffs and rocks, and these only during the breeding season.

It is a nice inoffensive sort of bird, and how the species has managed to increase on the Saltee Island so much in the last twenty years is a puzzle to me.

Young guillemot and egg, Saltee Island.

It lays one egg. If the egg comes to grief it will lay another, but it only hatches out one chick. It lays this egg on the bare rock, no attempt at a nest being made. If the egg is laid on a very narrow ledge the bird may knock it off when rising to fly, but if the ledge is broad the egg, although disturbed, will not roll off. The reason for this is that the shape of the egg and its centre of gravity are such that when pushed it does not roll straight but describes a narrow circle.

Many eggs are lost in this fashion, but the principal casualties are caused by robbery, both by man and the herring gull. Previous to the Irish Free State Act for the Protection of Birds dealers came from England and carried away boat-loads of the guillemots' eggs, which exhibit such a variety of markings that they are prized by collectors. So systematic was this wholesale robbery that the numbers of guillemots declined rapidly in the years immediately prior to the war. Since then, thanks to the watchfulness of the Irish police, they have increased, and the principal losses are due to the depredations of the herring gull, which bird, I may mention, is not protected in the Irish Free State. I have watched one of these gulls steal the egg from between the legs of a guillemot and carry it in its beak, large though it was, to a flat rock where it broke it. Then having eaten the contents, it proceeded to steal another, continuing the process until its voracious appetite was satisfied. But this robber is not always content with stealing eggs. I have seen a gull take a guillemot chick and tear it asunder before its mother's eyes. The unfortunate guillemot seems defenceless against the herring gull; it gets so flustered that its attempt to protect its offspring is of little avail against the bold raids of the robber.

Guillemots, Saltee Island. Note bird (centre) with fish.

Guillemots with eggs on cliff, Saltee Island.

The Razorbill

The razorbill differs little from the guillemot. The latter has a sharp-pointed bill, but the razorbill, as its name suggests, has a broad bill with which it can draw blood. The guillemot uses its bill like a rapier, and the razorbill in the manner of a cavalry sword. Like its cousin it lays a single large egg but it deposits it under a rock or in some crevice.

Once when lecturing to Boy Scouts I asked them the old riddle, 'Why does a razorbill raise her bill?' The correct answer is, 'So that the sea urchin can see her chin,' but having asked the riddle I realised that I had completely forgotten the answer and was forced to improvise with, 'Because the sea urchin was searchin(g) for her,' a particularly loathsome attempt but better than appearing an absolute idiot to a group of keen youngsters.

We were fortunate enough to see part of the education of a young razorbill; it was no namby-pamby process. The parents evidently thought that the youngster was old enough to learn how to fend for himself. So far life had been a dream to him – plenty of fish without the trouble of catching them, basking in the sunshine on nice warm rocks, and when night came with its chilly air he was warmed and cuddled by an affectionate mother.

The chick was now in the adolescent stage, plump and fat, most of his down replaced by feathers, but he had never flown nor had he ever been in or on his true element, the sea; He was timid and feared to launch himself into the great space. He refused, in spite of the solicitations of his father and mother, to leave the safety of terra firma. Trembling, he stood on the edge of the cliff like a timid bather who fears to plunge. The parents consulted together. I can imagine their conversation: 'We cannot allow our child to disgrace us; are we not good and true razorbills, have we not chased fish, and braved the storms on the sea, have we failed in any of the qualities that are expected in our breed? Where, oh where, did he get the yellow streak of cowardice?' 'I am sure,' says father, 'he did not inherit it from me.' 'He certainly did not get it from my family,' says his mother.

Razorbills, Saltee Island.

'What is to be done?' say both of them. The matter is decided promptly. Mother, or more probably father, pushes him over the edge. The cliff is a hundred feet high; the sea seems so far away; he endeavours to use his wings, but, as he has never flown previously, his attempts are pathetic – they serve, however, to break the rapidity of his descent as he falls on the surface of the sea and raises a big splash. His thick coating of fat serves as a shock-absorber and he emerges to the surface looking none the worse.

One would think that now he would be left alone to recover from the effects of his terrifying experience, but no! his education in the environment in which he will spend his life has yet to take place. He is unwilling to dive below the surface of the water, so father and mother and many of their neighbours chase him and peck at him until in sheer desperation he tries to escape from his tormentors by diving. This is repeated over and over again until at last he begins to feel confidence in his new surroundings and gains the respite which he has earned.

He has yet to be taught how to capture his own food and his parents help to feed him until in a week or two he is able to live by his own efforts.

Gulls

Four varieties of gulls inhabit the island: the herring gull, the kittiwake, the great black back and the lesser black back.

To see the herring gull standing on the cliffs in sunshine one would imagine him to be an emblem of purity, but he is only awaiting his opportunity for robbery, and the purity of his white breast is like unto a whitened sepulchre. He has, however, one redeeming feature; like all wild creatures he is very solicitous for the welfare of his young.

When one approaches the vicinity of their nest the parents rise in the air uttering the warning cry which tells the young birds of danger and the cries never cease until the intruder is at a safe distance. When the young birds hear the warning note they 'freeze' and remain still until danger is past. So close do they squat and so invisible are they, by reason of their mottled colouring, that I have more than once walked on a young bird that I did not see.

This obedience to the parents' warning is a strongly developed instinct. I have seen young birds only a few days old, and also big birds able to fly, remain immobile whilst I gazed at them at a distance of only a couple of yards.

The young of the black backs adopt a similar attitude, and on several occasions I have been attacked by a parent great black back who swooped down to within a few feet of my head. The great black back is a large bird with a wing-spread of several feet; his beak is powerful, and as I did not like his attentions at such close quarters I put on motor-goggles and a hat as protection.

One may describe the herring gull as a cunning thief or pickpocket, but the great black back is more aptly described as a pirate or a buccaneer. He does not bother about larceny, but commits murder in the grand fashion. I have seen him swoop down on a puffin and disembowel it whilst the unfortunate victim was still alive. He kills other birds and includes in his bill of fare rabbits and other creatures.

The herring gull nests everywhere on the island, mostly in large colonies, and makes a tidy, well-built nest, but the great black back makes what one can hardly call a nest, on a high place with a commanding outlook and removed from other birds, including those of his own species – precautions which are possibly the result of an evil conscience.

He is difficult to photograph, so we erected a hiding-tent decorated with bracken near his nest, in the hope that we might be successful. 'We did not approach the tent for several days, but we could see through our field-glasses that the parents did not occupy the vantage-point that they had frequented previous to the erection of the tent. In despair we put entrails of rabbit on the rock, but the birds evidently thought this was a trap and refused to touch them.

Nearly a week had passed when we noticed that the birds were back in their old quarters. It was the day on which we had planned to leave the island and the boat was to call that evening for us, so we determined to make the attempt.

Birds are bad mathematicians: they cannot count, so we relied on this fact. Three of us went into the tent and after a few minutes my two sons came out

Young herring gull, Saltee Island.

and went away from the district, leaving me the sole occupant. Before they left I had cut a small slit in the cloth through which I could insert the lens of my camera.

Even with these precautions it was four hours before the birds came back. I had given up hope, and as time for our departure drew nigh I packed up my camera and was about to leave when I heard a noise outside. Peering carefully through the slit I saw a wonderful scene. One of the parent birds had a large fish, with portions of which it was feeding the chick, while the other parent was standing in close attendance giving voice to contented mutterings. It was an intimate picture of family life, and ideally situated from a photographic viewpoint.

Hurriedly I unpacked the camera, but I was too late. By the time the camera was ready the birds had got behind a rock, where they were protected from the cool east wind. I had lost a unique picture and only managed to get a photograph of one of the adult birds.

The kittiwake is my favourite gull; it is inoffensive to other birds and yet it is chivalrous and brave when the necessity arises. It builds on ledges of the cliffs or on boulders projecting from the clay overhanging the sea. It gets its name from its cry, which it exactly resembles. I have watched for hours these pretty birds flying in graceful circles near their homes, occasionally uttering their plaintive cry which is so different from that of the herring gull, which is discordant, and from that of the black back, which is a deep bass.

They have a strong community sense, for if a herring gull tries to rob one of their

Kittiwake gulls and nests, Saltee Island.

Kittiwake gulls on nest, Saltee Island.

nests the defence is not left to the unfortunate victim of the raid – the kittiwake is much smaller and individually would be no match for the large herring gull – but all the neighbours rise from their nests and mob the intruder. I have never seen a herring gull successful in one of the attempted robberies – a striking example of the old motto 'union is strength.'

Some ornithologists state that the incubation is shared by both sexes but I have never seen this occur. Always one of the birds sat on the eggs, which she only left occasionally to stretch her wings, and although the male was in the vicinity he never took her place.

They are extraordinarily affectionate birds. It is beautiful to watch the return of the male bird to his nesting mate; it is a true lovers' meeting. There is much cooing, they rub their bills together in a manner suggestive of a human kiss, and then the male regurgitates some partially digested fish, the mother opens her bill and father delicately inserts a choice morsel well down in her throat. The process is repeated, and after more demonstrations of affection father goes off to continue his active career of fishing. From lengthy observations I came to the conclusion that the male bird gave more food to his wife than he himself ate – a lesson in matrimonial etiquette that many humans would do well to ponder.

I wondered why the male bird did not bring whole fish to his wife, which is usual with most of the other birds, and can only conclude that the partially digested food with which he fed her was less liable to cause indigestion during the lengthy period of incubation, when she took no active exercise.

Oyster-catchers

Perhaps the most noisy of all the birds on the Saltee Island are the oyster-catchers or sea pies. Whenever anybody approaches within about fifty yards of their nest the parents rise in the air uttering a most piercing noise. If they kept quiet their young would be much safer, for usually, though not always, the nest consists of a hollow in the shingle with no lining; occasionally a few pieces of dry grass may be used but not enough to attract attention. The mottling of the eggs and the markings of the young birds blend so harmoniously with the surrounding stones that it is extremely hard to spot them. On more than one occasion I have had the greatest difficulty in finding a nest which I had previously seen and to which I had returned in order to photograph it.

Once when I was occupied in this search the mother bird tried to lure me away from her young by feigning a broken wing which she dragged along the ground, never allowing me to get close enough to capture her, and all the time leading me farther and farther away from the young birds. When I returned to the nest I could find only one of the chicks – the other two had completely vanished.

These birds live principally on limpets, which they remove from the rocks at low tide, and the empty shells which are always found near the nest provide a clue to its whereabouts.

The oyster-catcher is a handsome bird with powerful orange-coloured bill and a black and white plumage. The name is a corruption of a continental word that has nothing to do with oysters, the shells of which I have never seen amongst the debris of its meals.

The Cormorant

The least attractive of all sea birds are the cormorants. In their breeding haunts they are actually repulsive. They breed in colonies, making large untidy nests of dried seaweed and the stench in hot weather is almost overpowering; the combined odour of rotten fish and excreta is past description. They seem to have no redeeming features; they are infested with lice and are arrant cowards, deserting their young at the slightest hint of danger.

In the illustration below one sees a young bird with neck extended as if he were engaged in singing but, as a matter of fact, he is so nervous that this extension of his neck is merely preliminary to vomiting a fish about ten inches long. How he managed to swallow such a large fish appears almost a miracle, for its tail must have projected into the lower portion of his neck. As we passed along the edge of the cliffs where the cormorants nested we noticed that we were followed at a safe distance by some herring gulls. Observation through our field-glasses revealed the fact that when the young cormorants, who were afflicted with nerves by our presence, became ill, the herring gulls swooped down and stole the fish which they had vomited.

Young cormorants, Saltee Island.

Strange to say, the cormorant has a place in literature.

Milton in *Paradise Lost* makes Satan take the form of a cormorant in the following lines:

> Thence up he flew and on the tree of life
> The middle tree and the highest there that grew,
> Sat like a cormorant; yet not true life
> Thereby regained, but sat devising death
> To them who lived; nor on the virtue thought
> Of that life-giving plant, but only used
> For prospect, what, well used, had been the pledge
> Of immortality.

When I first read these lines I thought that Milton had blundered in his natural history, but since then I have seen cormorants nesting in trees on an island in a lake in County Galway. One would not think it possible that a marine bird, with feet like a cormorant, could perch on a branch.

A writer in *Punch* has written an ode to a cormorant.

To A Cormorant

> There at the dawn thou sunnest thee,
> Spreading thy wings to the cleansing air,
> Lulled to sleep by the singing sea,
> Crammed with herrings and void of care;
>
> Surely the writers have done thee wrong,
> Dubbing thine appetites unrefined;
> Others keep at it the whole day long,
> Not, like thee, when they feel inclined;
>
> Guillemots guzzle and seagulls stuff;
> Ceasing never they search the seas;
> Thou dost sit, when thou'st had enough,
> Lapped apart in reflective ease.
>
> Sage, philosopher, altruist–
> These were ever the angler's role,
> Whether he fishes with beak or wrist,
> Whether he hooks them, or wolfs 'em whole.
>
> And would, like thee, I were all these things,
> Could sit out there where the white rock gleams,
> With the bright sun warming my outstretched wings,
> Digesting herrings and dreaming dreams!
>
> Algol
[Cyril Herbert Bretherton]

The Peregrine Falcon

In a book of this character space does not permit of detailed descriptions of all the birds, but I cannot omit to mention the peregrine falcon, that fine bold bird of prey. For many years it nested on the island but continual robbing of its eggs drove it away. I only hope that the protection which it now enjoys will tempt it back to the island, for although I have seen the nests of the peregrine in different parts of the country I have never been able to observe it so well as when on the Saltee Island.

The peregrine is the bird that was used in the days of falconry and the Arabs still use it for this sport. Although a bird of prey, he showed himself a gentleman for he did not molest his neighbours. When the larder required replenishing he captured his food on the other side of the island, away, so to speak, from his home town. This may have been only due to clever policy, but if so it shows a high degree of intelligence, for even mankind prefer to live at peace with their immediate neighbours.

The Manx Shearwater

When last on the Saltee I thought at first that the Manx shearwater had deserted the island, but happening to stay up late one night at photographic operations I heard it. Listening on the following nights to their weird calls I was astonished at the regularity in time of their homecoming. Every night at twelve-twenty, summer time in early July, the first cry was heard and the last was heard almost exactly thirty minutes later.

Although the birds are the great attraction of the island they are not the only one. The wild flowers are wonderful. When the wild hyacinths bloom one sees acres of these beautiful blue blossoms. To reach parts of the cliff one has to walk through them and when doing so I always had a guilty feeling as if I were committing a sacrilege. Later in the season the sea pinks and bladder campion and rock plants gladden the eye with a glorious profusion. The greater part of the south side of the island is covered with sea pinks and the western portion is a mass of the bell-shaped flowers of the campion. The ground is literally a carpet of flowers. No description can do justice to the picture; it must be seen.

Although I have visited the island many times, the occasion on which I was accompanied by my wife and family stands out prominently – the weather was fine, there was perfect harmony, everything (except the picture of the great black back) went according to plan, and as I sat in the boat on our return journey I thought of the scene in the Forest of Arden:

> And thus our life exempt from public haunt
> Finds tongues in trees,
> Books in the running brooks,
> Sermons in stones,
> And good in everything.
>
> *As You Like It*
> William Shakespeare

Chapter Seventeen

Conclusion

To my thinking one of the most disturbing features of modern life is the constant whirl of speed, excitement and competition in which so many people live, move and have their being, and the disinclination or inability of the younger generation to occupy their spare time in the simpler, more beautiful and more lasting pleasures which can be obtained by the observation of the world of nature.

The game of golf was at one time a recreation which kept in the open air men who might otherwise occupy themselves at less healthy pursuits. I may say that I do not play golf. I am not old enough. I have plenty of other and better hobbies and, as I have said, I do not regard golf as a game. It is a disease which is especially virulent when it attacks middle-aged men. I have friends, however, who do play golf and they complain that they cannot get a game on a Saturday afternoon unless they enter for a competition.

This spirit of excessive competition seems to be eating into every phase of human activity and is destroying that contemplative faculty which has produced the great thinkers and scientists and philosophers throughout the ages. The price of all this feverishness must be paid in the future and it will be a high price.

The remedy lies largely with the parents and the teachers and they have a tremendous responsibility. I have never known a youth who was interested in field natural history to 'go wrong.' I am not so foolish as to suggest that the study of nature is a remedy for all the ills of modern life, but I will say that it would be a big step in the right direction.

Last year, when recuperating from a severe illness, I sat by myself on a camp chair outside my bungalow in the Dublin hills. I had field glasses and a book, but I had no need to open the latter. I was not lonely, for in two hours I observed ten different varieties of butterflies and saw or heard seventeen different kinds of birds.

The interests which I formed in youth have been an inexhaustible treasure and joy to me and I thank God for the Providence which directed my thoughts to the contemplation of the beauty and wonders of His world which lie at our very doors.

Symposium of island life. Currach on supports, ass with turf creels, woman spinning, Inishbofin,

INDEX

Entries in **Bold** indicate an illustration.

Achill Head   56, **56**
Achill Island   15, 51-61; antiquities 60; Cathedral Rocks **58**, 59; cottage, modern **52**; cottage, traditional **51**, 52; Minaun Cliffs   56, **57**, **58**
Alcohol   16, 21-22, 106
Antiquarian Handbook   13, 71
Antrim, County   20
Aran Islands *see also* Inishere, Inismaan, Inismore   8, 16, 18, 77-122, 123; antiquities 89-101; beaches 85; bird life 117; boys clothing 97; cliffs **76**, 85, 91-92, **91**; climate 85; clothing 97; currach 32, 37, 38, **40**, **41**; dancing 104; description of islanders 94, **95**; fields 'gardens' **82**, 83, **84**, 86; government housing 106; housing description 107; mass 101; match-making 105-106; primitive oil lamp 106; soil creation/ land making **82**, 83, **84**, 94; spinning 116; wake 106; walls **83**; wedding 105
Aran of the Saints   78
Aranmore Island   12
Arranged marriage   105-106
Asses *see* Donkeys
Atlantis   92
Auks   153, 154, 157

B.T. Batsford Ltd   10
Ballinderry No. 2 Crannoge   13, 34
Balor   26, 27
Barrett, John   60
Basket-making   110, 115, 117, **117**
Baskets, Creel, Kisaun, Ribh, Skib   91, 104, 109, 110, 111, 117
Basking Shark   68, 106
Beehive Cells   46, 92, 144
Beginish   123, 129
Belfast   20
Bird Sanctuary   19, 149-151
Bishop's Rock, Inishbofin   72
Black and Tans   74, 151
Black Head   78
Blackpool   16
Blarney Stone   53
Blasket Islands *see also* Great Blasket Island   16, 123-138, 140; currach 37, **37**, 38, **42**; spinning 116
Board of Works   29, 45, 46
Bog Butter   27
Booley migration   60
Boreens   83, 86, **86**
Bosco's Castle   72
Boycott, Captain   53
Brambles   73, 104, 110
Bran, Finn Mcumhail's dog   88
Brian Boru   127
British Museum   123
Bronze Age   20, 47, 73, 77
Bruce, King Robert   20
Bruce's Castle Rathlin Island   20
Burke, Sir Richard   64

Cahir Island   68
Castledermot   30
Cathedral Rocks   **58**, 59
Cattle   52, 73, 83, 85, 91, 111, 113, 115, 136; Shipping to mainland 111-115, **113**, **114**, 136-138, **137**
Celtic (Irish) Church   15, 29, 30, 144; bells 29
Chevaux-de-frise   89, **89**
Choughs   74, 117, 147
Chrismatory   46
Christ's Saddle   140, 146
Christian Missionary   27, 44, 71, 78, 99
Church, Ban on Poteen   21
Civic Guard *see* Police
Clare Island   53, 56, 63-69, 73; Abbey 65; cliffs **62**; cultivation 65; currach 38; lack of antiquities 69
Clare, County   30, 77, 78, 79, 80
Cleggan   71
Clew Bay   63
Clifden Races   74
Clocha-breaca *see also* cursing stones   45
Clonfert, Bishop of   72
Columbus, Christopher   34
Commissioners of Irish Lights   24, 140
Cong   77
Congested Districts Board   29, 52
Connemara   51, 56, 80, 104
Cook, Brian   10
Coptic Church   30
Coracle   32, 33
Corcaguiney   123
Cormorant   162, **162**
Courtesy of Islanders   16, 17, 23, 52, 53, 61
Covenanters   72
Cradle   **108**, 109
Creel   91, 104, 109, 110, 111, 117

Criss (Belt)   **96**, 97
Croagh Martin   136
Croaghaun   **55**, 56
Cromwell, Oliver   18, 72
Cromwellian period   71, 72, 77, 98
Currach   59, 60, 63, 68, 69, 74, 79, 85, 111, 113, 121, 123, 135; Aran 32, 37, 38; Blasket 37, **37**, 38, **42**; building 33, 117; Clare Island 38; ease of repair 38, **73**; hides 33; Inishark Island 38; Inishbofin Island 38; load carrying 39, **39**, 85, 136, **137**, 138; Rossguill Peninsular **36**, 37; sally rods 33; seaworthyness 38; tarred canvas 33, 37, 38; Tory Island 34, **35**, **40**; transporting animals 38, **39**, 113, 136, **137**, 138
Cursing Stones   15, 29, 45, **45**, 46, 100
Cyclists Touring Club   51

Dalkey, Island   18, 19
Dardanelles   60
Dhu Caher   92
Dhugan (Dugan) Family of Tory   27-28
Dingle   135
Dodds, Mr A.   13
Dog names in Ireland   88
Donal na Neelough   131
Donegal, County   21, 23, 27, 29
Donkey (Asses)   43, 53, 66, 69, 86, **87**, 88, **111**, **128**, 134, 135, **165**
Dooagh   **55**
Down, County   24
Dublin   15, 18, 28, 30, 50, 56, 65, 79, 85, 104, 122, 135, 150
Dublin, County   19
Dug-out canoe   13, 33
Dugort Strand   **55**
Dugort   59
Dun Aengus   **76**, 89-91, **89**, **90**
Dun Conor   77
Dun Conor   77, 92, 94
Dun Moher   92
Dun Oghil   92
Dun Onacht   92
Dunquin   124
Dysert O'Dea, cross of   30

Easter   143, 144
Elizabeth I, Queen, 63, 65
Elizabethan Period   20, 27, 60, 71
Emigration   18, 23, 85, 127
English Crown Forces   20, 27
English Government   64
English language   24; origin of 'Boycott' 53
Eye testing   60

Faherty, Kate   88
Fairies   27, 97, 121
Fascination of Islands   15
Finn Mcumhail   88
Firbolgs   77
Fire, destroys Mason collection   8
Fishery, protection   79-80
Fishing,   38, 51, 79, 80, 121; cliff 91, **91**; lobster 21, 37, 43, 69, 71, 121, 135; salmon 33, 60
Flaherty. Robert   105, 106
Flash Photography   99, 128
Fleetwood   80
Flint Tools   20, 77
Flower, Dr Robin   12, 123, 129, 134
Fog-signal Station   143
Fogarty, Dr   13
Fomorians   26
Ford,   51; Model A   7; Model T   7, 151; V8   7
Fulmars   142, 147

Gaelic *also* Irish Language   24, 44, 79, 85, 104, 119, 131, 136
Gaeltacht   24
Galway Bay   77

166

Galway Fair   16, 111
Galway,   7, 34, 78, 85, 113, 121
Galway, County   8, 21, 123, 163
Gannets   142, 147, 148
Geddes, Mr A.M.   13
Geese   66, 68
Gilbert and Sulliven   140
Glasgow   24, 56
Glencolumbkille   28
Goats   60, 143
Gold Standard   30
Golf   165
Government Supplied Boats   33, 38
Granuaile, *see* O'Malley, Grace
Granuaile's Castle   63, **64**, 68
Great Black Back Gull   158
Great Blasket Island   123, **123**, 125; attending mass 134; Great Blasket Island, cottages **126**, 127, **127**; cultivation 136; dun/fort 136; funeral 134; harbour 124; islander's clothing 130, **130**; king 124; population 136; winter supplies 124
Great Saltee Island   7, 149-153, **149**; bird population 12
Greek Cross   46, 49
Gregorian Calendar   143
Grey, Lord Deputy   128
Guillemots   147, 154, **155**, **156**

Hares   60, 68
Harvard University Archaeological Mission   13, 34
Herring Gull   155, 158, **159**; photographing 158
High Island   74
HMS *Wasp*   29
Holy Well   49, 73
Horses   24, **25**, 33, 53, **61**, 66, **68**, 69, 74, 78, **82**, 83, 86, **86**, **88**, 113, 135
Hy Brasil   13, 92, **93**

Ice Age   30, 80
Illicit Distilling   21, **22**
In Search of Ireland   3
Inishark Island   72, 74; currach 38
Inishbofin Island   38, 71-74, **70**, **72**, **165**; ancient graveyard 73; bird life 74; old church ('the Monastery') 72; population 73
Inishere Island *see also* Aran Islands   79, 119-122; antiquities 119; church of St. Keevan 121; forts 94; graveyard **120**, 121; lack of harbour 79; priest 101; transport on 86
Inishmaan Island *see also* Aran Islands   77, **77**, **88**, 111; cottages **102**; forts 92; lack of harbour 113; novelty of radio 103; transport on 86; waiting for steamer **112**
Inishmore Island *see also* Aran Islands   18, 78, **78**, 79, 80, 89, 103; Christian antiquities 98;

forts   92; glacial boulders 81; making land **82**, **84**; novelty of radio 103; transport on   86; wayside monuments 101, **102**
Inishmurray Island   27, 28, 29, 43-50; antiquities 43, 44; barrenness 43; bodies found washed onshore 44; cashel 46; evacuation 12; graveyard 44; mistaken for submarine 43; monastic settlement **15**; pilgrims 50; schoolmistress 43; sweat house **48**, 49; Women's Stone 47, **47**
Iona   27, 44
Ireland's Eye   19
Irish Civil War   9, 74, 150
Irish Government   24, 52, 53, 79, 85, 106, 127, 134; censorship 134
Irish Hospital Sweepstake   130
Irish Language   24, 44, 79, 85, 104, 119, 131, 136
Irish Potato Famine   68
Iron Age   77
Islands of Ireland   9, 10
Isle of Man   16, 78

Jelly-fish   153

Kean, Mrs.   124, **124**
Keel   51, 53, **54**, 56, 60
Keel Bay   **59**
Keem Bay   **58**
Kells   30
Kerry Mountains   16, 142
Kerry, County   98, 123
Killarney   56
Killeany   79, 98
Kilmore Quay   149, 151
Kilmurvey   89, 100, 103, 106
Kilnaboy   30
Kilronan   79, 80, 98, 116
Kilronan Fair   115
Kingsley, Charles   128
Kisaun   117
Kittiwakes   142, 158, 159-161, **160**
Klaasen, Cor   10
Knightstown Harbour   139
Knitting   79, 94, 116
Knockmore   63, **64**

Lambay Island   12, 19, 20, 27
Land Commission   69
Land War   69
Lanes, Aran, Boreens   83, 86, **86**
Latin   49
Lawrence collection   8
Lawrence of Dublin   7
Leitrim, County   78
Lesser Black Back Gull   158
Lighthouse   28, 139, 140, 143, 148
Lime burning   30, **31**
Limestone   19, 30, 77, 80; landscape   81, 83, **84**
Limpets   30, 121, 151, 161
Lindbergh, Charles   135
Lindisfarne   71
Little Skellig   139, **142**, 147; landing   148

Liverpool   56
Lloyd George, David   3, 53, 144
Lobster fishery   21, 37, 43, 69, 71, 121, 135; price of lobster catch 71
Lodging on the islands   18
London   15, 51, 65, 104, 135
Londonderry   28
Lorraine, Duke of   72
Lord Deputy of Ireland   64, 128
Lough Corrib   64
Louisburgh   63
Lugh   26

Mahr, Dr. A.   34
Man of Aran   105
Manx Shearwater   19, 164; unnerving cries   19
Marconi Direction Finding Station 24
Maroon (rockets)   143
Martin, Dr. Cecil   77
Mason Technology Limited   3
Mason, Alex   7, 8
Mason, Thomas Holmes   3; early photographs   7
Mayo, County   77
Mc Donagh, Mrs.   12, 103
Mecredy, R.J.   51
Midden   **120**, 121
Midges   51, 52
Milltown Races   79
Minaun Cliffs   56, **57**, **58**
Monasterboice   30
Moone   30
Morton, HV   3
Mount Brandon   128
Mount Eagle   128
Mourne Mountains   24
Moytura, Battle of   77
Muckish   27
Mullen, Pat   105
Myths and Legends of the Celtic Race 26

Napoleonic Fort   19
National Museum   30, 33, 34, 109, 121
Needle's Eye   **144**
Neolithic Remains   20
New York   56
Newgrange   47, 73
Norman Invasion   18

O'Connell, Daniel   131
O'Crohan, Thomas   12, 134
O'Donnell Clan   27, 53
O'Driscoll, Florence   140
O'Malley Clan   63
O'Malley, Grace   53, 60, 63, 65, 66, 72; burial place   65
O'Neill Clan   43
O'Neill Henken, Dr H.   13, 34
Oatquarter   78
Omey Island   74, **75**
Oral Traditions   26, 44
Osiers   117
Otters   60, 68
Our Lady of the Rosary   129
Oyster-catchers   161

167

Pampooties **96**, 97
Paradise Lost 163
Paris 104
Pearse, Patrick 127
Peat *see* turf 23
Pension 53, 94, 116
Peregrine Falcons 19, 147, **152**, 153, 164
Photographs of Islanders 18, 94
Picts 44
Pigs 111, 115
Pilgrims 50, 143
Pirates 27, 72
Plato 92
Police, Civic Guards 21, 22, 27, 29, 68, 69, 80, 135, 149, 153, 155
Pollock 59
Pookaun (wooden boat) 106
Postal Stamps 26
Postcards 3, 6; examples of 4, 5; hotels 8
Potatoes 38, 51, 83, 85, 110, 117, 138
Poteen 21-22
Prehistoric Man in Ireland 77
Priests, 72, 73, 101, 134; lack of 43, 136; transportation by Cromwell 72
Primroses 129
Puffins 147, **152**, 153

Quartz 73, 122
Queen of the Isles 63
Queenstown (Cobh) 56

Raleigh, Sir Walter 128
Rathlin Island 12, 20, 27
Rats 28, 44, 121, 150
Raven 19, 68
Razorbills **17**, 157, **157**
Revelstoke, Lord 19
Ribh 117, **117**
Robinson Crusoe 149, 151
Rolleston, T.W. 26
Roman Empire 18, 99
Roonah 63
Rossguill Peninsular Currach **36**, 37
Round Tower 29, **29**, 79, 98
Royal Academy, London 99
Royal Dublin Society 12
Royal Irish Constabulary *see* Police
Royal Society of Antiquaries of Ireland 49, 71

Sally (willow) rods 33, 37, 117
Salmon Fishery 33, 60
Saltee Island *see* Great Saltee Island
Saxon 20, 92
Scandinavian Place Names 18

Scotland 23, 27, 72
Scots, early mediaeval people 44
Scott, Professor J.A. 12
Scottish Coast 20
Seals 19, 68, 74
Seasonal farm work 51, 53
Seaweed harvesting 109-110, **110**, 118; dilisk 109; for manure 68, 69, 74, 86, 109, **111**; kelp burning 109, 110, **110**; tools 110
Seven Churches, the 98, 99, 100, 104; cross 100
Shag, lesser comorant 149
Sheep 27, 43, 56, 66, 79, 115, 130, 135, 136
Sheep-dog 60, 135
Shellfish fishery 71
Shipwrecks 24, 29, 130
Skellig islands *see also* Skellig Michael, Little Skellig 8, 139-148
Skellig Michael 16, 139, **139**, 140, **141**; Skellig Michael, cemetery **145**, 147; landing 139, 140; monastery 142, 144, **145**, 146-147; monastery steps **11**; Needle's Eye 143, **144**; oratories 147; St Michael's Pillar 143; well 147
Skib 117
Slea Head 128
Sleivemore **55**, 59, **61**
Sleivemore village 60
Slide Cart 24, **25**
Slieve Donagh 136
Sligo, County 43
Smerwick Harbour 128
Smuggling 22
Soda Bread 111
Soils 21, 23, 60, 83
Spanish Armada 47, 129
Spinning **31**, 68, 109, **109**, 115, 116, **127**
Spiritual quality of islands 16
St, Michael's Pillar 143, **143**
St. Anthony's (Egyptian) Cross 30
St. Brendan 34
St. Brigid's Cross 109
St. Christopher 63
St. Colman 71
St. Columba, *see* St. Colmcille
St. Columcille (Columba) 27, 43, 44, 109; banishes rats 28, 44; battle with St. Finian 44; segregation of female sex 44
St. Enda 78
St. Finian 43, 44
St. Gall 99
St. Keevan, church of, Inishere **120**, 121
St. Malo 71
St. McDara's Day 100

St. Michael's Church 146
St. Molaise 43, 44, 47
St. Nicholas of Galway, church of 34
St. Patrick 109
St. Peter and Paul, Feast of 100
Stormy Petrels 147
Streedagh 50
Submarine, Inishmurray mistaken for 43
Summer Time 144
Sybil Head 128
Sydney, Sir Henry 63
Synge, J.M. 17

Taxes 135
Teach Molaise 47
Teampul Benen 98
Teampul Brecain 98
Teampul na Teinidh 47, **48**
Tearaght 139, 140
The Islandman 134
Three Sisters 128
Torry Island,
Tory Clay 28
Tory Island 23-31, 33, 34; antiquities 29; cliffs **23**, 24; crossing 23; currach 34, **35**, **40**; denudation of soil 23; dun 27; home-made tools 24, **25**; king 26; longevity of Islanders 24; pronounciation 23; using shipwreck materials 24; landing-stage 30; T cross 29, 30
Tourism 51; problems of 16
Triskelion symbol 78
Turf 23, 30, 43, **54**, 86, 104, 111, 123, **128**, 131, 134
Twelve Pins of Connemara 71, 85

United States of America 18, 23, 60, 85, 105, 106, 130

Valentia Island 139, 148
Vicarstown 129
Venice 16, 134
Viking Raids 18, 29, 30, 43, 146

Wakeman, Mr. W. F. 44, 49
Waters, Mrs 43
Weaving 68, 115, 116, **116**
Westport 60, 63
Westropp, T.J. 71, 92, 140
Westward Ho! 128
Wexford, County 149
Wild Birds Protection Act 149, 155
William III, King 72
Wooden Utensils **108**, 109
Wool 68, 79, 94, 97, 115, 130